"*Paradise Lost: A Poetic Journey* is a poetic retelling of salvation history through the lens of John Milton's *Paradise Lost*. The exquisite poetry takes the reader from the depths of sin and hell to the glory of redemption when God will wipe every tear from our eyes (Rev 21:4)."

—MATTHEW EYERMAN, pastor, Blessed Maria Gabriella Church

"John Milton's epic biblical poem *Paradise Lost* finds a new fresh voice in Paul Buchheit's version, eloquently articulating both the poetic form and compelling story of Milton's classic work. This is a great find for anyone who would love to enjoy this epic poem, unencumbered by the need to continually reference footnotes for definitions of the more archaic vocabulary, classical and mythological inferences."

—NICHOLAS ZOOK, pastor, Concordia Church

"This book stands as a condensed alternative to Milton's mighty *Paradise Lost*. If you are a commoner (not a theologian, philosopher, poet, playwright, etc.) who wants to familiarize yourself with/enjoy this classic, this is just the right version to read! It will treat you to some fine poetry and allow you to enjoy the complete story without missing any important detail. So, without any hesitation, I recommend you read it!"

—RAJU CHACKO, *Reedsy*

"*Paradise Lost: A Poetic Journey* easily manages to bend its genre in an even more remarkable way, and its poetic entries will easily resonate with readers from all walks of life and ages. The skillfully delivered dialogues and the wily changes in tone laud the key message that the poet seeks to deliver, and that rings true throughout. Through these complex and wonderful poems, God's unyielding love for humankind shines, and Milton's previous work that these poems are based upon receives much justice."

—LILY ANDREWS, *Feathered Quill*

"Those who like horror-themed poetry and fiction will appreciate this book. Additionally, those who are intrigued by the philosophical elements of the original *Paradise Lost* and similar works will likely enjoy the journey this book offers."

—NICOLE YURCABA, *The US Review of Books*

Paradise Lost

Paradise Lost
A Poetic Journey

PAUL BUCHHEIT

RESOURCE *Publications* · Eugene, Oregon

PARADISE LOST
A Poetic Journey

Copyright © 2024 Paul Buchheit. All rights reserved. Except for brief quotations in critical publications or reviews, no part of this book may be reproduced in any manner without prior written permission from the publisher. Write: Permissions, Wipf and Stock Publishers, 199 W. 8th Ave., Suite 3, Eugene, OR 97401.

Resource Publications
An Imprint of Wipf and Stock Publishers
199 W. 8th Ave., Suite 3
Eugene, OR 97401

www.wipfandstock.com

PAPERBACK ISBN: 979-8-3852-1079-4
HARDCOVER ISBN: 979-8-3852-1080-0
EBOOK ISBN: 979-8-3852-1081-7

04/16/24

Doré, Gustav, illustrator. *John Milton's Paradise Lost*. New York: Peter Fenelon Collier, 1866. Also from Milton, John. *Milton's Paradise Lost, illustrated by Gustave Doré* London & New York, Cassell, Petter, and Galpin, 1866.

Blake, William. *Illustrations to Milton's "Paradise Lost"* The Butts Set, 1808

(Note: Images by Doré are identified by Book and Line numbers. Images by Blake are identified by name.)

Contents

Introduction | xiii

1 | Satan and His Allies are Banished to Hell

Author's Plea | *Iambic Tetrameter* | 3
Angels Rebel, and Are Cast Into Hell | *Anapestic Tetrameter* | 4
Satan Plots Revenge | *Decima* | 6
Beelzebub Questions Satan | *Shakespearean Sonnet* | 7
Satan Frees Himself | *Iambic Tri-, Tetra- meter* | 8
Satan Seeks His Captive Allies | *Octave* | 9
The Demon Warrior | *Quatrain* | 10
The Devils Are Rallied | *Iambic Hexameter Sonnet* | 12
Devil Leaders | *Iambic Tetrameter* | 14
More Devil Rebels | *Heroic Rispetto* | 16
Devils Roused Again | *Bref Double* | 18
Pandemonium | *Anapestic Tetrameter* | 20

2 | The Demons Plan a Strategy to Gain Vengeance on God. Satan Begins His Journey to Earth.

Satan Addresses His Army of Demons | *Octave* | 25
More Exhortation | *Quintilla* | 26
The Princes of War, Politics, and Greed Speak | *Iambic Pentameter* | 28

Contents

Beelzebub Talks About the Destruction of Man | *Iambic Heptameter* | 30
Preparing for a Flight through Chaos | *Kyrielle* | 32
The Demons Gather for Satan's Departure | *Espinela* | 33
A View of Chaos | *Iambic Nonameter* | 34
The State of Hell During Satan's Departure | *Iambic Hexameter* | 35
Satan Approaches the Gates at the Edge of Hell | *Iambic Tetrameter* | 37
Satan Meets a Woman-Snake and an Amorphous Shape | *Rime Couee* | 40
Satan Has Encountered Sin and Death | *Shakespearean Sonnet* | 41
Satan is Released into the Abyss | *Iambic Tetra-, Octa- meter* | 43

3 | As Heaven Watches, Satan Sneaks into Paradise

Prologue to Light: The Author Implores God for Wisdom | *Petrarchan Sonnet* | 49
God the Father and Son Foretell Man's Redemption | *Iambic Hexameter* | 51
Song of Judgment | *Common Meter* | 53
The Angels Rejoice | *Dactylic Heptameter* | 54
Satan Flies through Chaos toward the Earth | *Iambic Pentameter* | 56
Jacob's Ladder | *Terza Rima* | 57
An Angel Appears | *Rispetto* | 59
Satan Disguises Himself as a Cherub | *Iambic Hendecameter* | 60
Satan Deceives the Angel | *Iambic Hexameter* | 61

4 | Satan Draws Closer to God's Children in Eden

Satan Questions Himself | *Sonnet* | 65
Satan's Soliloquy: Bemoaning His Plight | *Nazm* | 67
Satan is Overwhelmed by Eden's Beauty | *Iambic Tetrameter* | 69

Contents

Eve and Adam in the Garden of Eden | *Anapestic Pentameter* | 72
Satan Laments the Couple's Good Fortune | *Shakespearean Sonnet* | 75
Angels Confer about Satan's Deceit | *Common Meter* | 77
An Idyllic Evening for Adam and Eve | *Cyhydedd Fer* | 79
A Night for Eden's Lovers | *Sonnet* | 81
Satan Stalks Eve, and Argues with the Angel Gabriel | *Iambic Hexameter* | 83

5 | After Eve Suffers a Bad Dream, Raphael is Sent by God to Warn the Couple of Satan's Treachery, and to Explain the Downfall of Rebellious Angels

Eve Has a Troubling Dream | *Iambic Pentameter* | 89
Eve and Adam Wake Up to the Grandeur of Eden | *Iambic Trimeter* | 92
God Sends Raphael to Earth to Warn the Couple | *Anapestic Nonameter* | 93
Raphael Dines with Adam and Eve | *Iambic Pentameter* | 97
Adam Questions Raphael | *Octave* | 100
Raphael Advises Adam | *Quintilla* | 101
Raphael Begins to Recount the Fall of the Angels | *Iambic Decameter* | 103
Sonnet to the Angels Celebrating the Son of God | *Sonnet* | 104
Raphael Recalls the Downfall of Rebellious Angels | *Common Meter* | 105
Satan Rallies His Rebel Cohorts | *Anapestic Heptameter* | 106

6 | Raphael Continues His Story. He Describes the War between Angels and Demons.

Ábdiel Returns to Heaven to Report on Satan's Treachery | *Dactylic Pentameter* | 109
Angels and Devils Prepare for Battle | *Iambic Pentameter* | 110
Satan and Abdiel Argue | *Anapestic Tetrameter* | 113

Contents

The Battle Begins with Satan and Michael in the Lead | *Iambic Hexameter* | 115
An Aside | *Heroic Stanza* | 116
The Demons Develop a New Weapon | *Trochaic Octameter* | 117
The Demons Deploy a Deadly Cannon | *Iambic Octameter* | 119
The Demon Army Anticipates Victory | *Anapestic Octameter* | 121
The Son of God Joins the Fray | *Iambic Pentameter* | 123
The Son of God Subdues the Enemy | *Common Meter* | 125
Celebration of a Merciful Triumph | *Rondeau* | 129

7 | The Story of Creation

The Author's Plea | *Octave* | 133
Raphael Answers Questions about God and Creation | *Ballade* | 134
Raphael Cautions Adam and Eve about Knowledge | *Octave* | 136
The Angel Begins to Explain the Universe | *Anapestic Hexameter* | 137
God Creates the Universe, Then Adds the Earth | *Iambic Tetrameter* | 138
God Makes Adjustments | *Quatrain* | 139
God Creates the First Animals | *Trochaic Heptameter* | 141
More Animals, Insects, and finally Man and Woman | *Iambic Trimeter* | 143
All Heaven Celebrates. Raphael Concludes His Story | *Chueh-Chu* | 145
Sonnet of Glory: Mankind Receives Gifts and Guidance | *Shakespearean Sonnet* | 146

8 | Adam and Raphael Finish Their Conversation. Adam Describes the Gifts from God: Paradise and a Female Partner.

Adam Asks Raphael about the Role of Earth | *Iambic Heptameter* | 151
Raphael Reflects | *Nonet* | 152

Contents

Adam Receives a Dreamlike Message from God | *Anapestic Pentameter* | 153
Adam Speaks to God about His Need for a Partner | *Shakespearean Sonnet* | 154
God Complies, and Creates Woman | *Shakespearean Sonnet* | 155
Raphael Warns Adam about Lustful Behavior | *Spenserian Stanza* | 157
Raphael's Parting Thoughts | *Haiku* | 158

9 | Eve and Adam's Disobedience

The Author's Lament | *Iambic Tetrameter* | 163
Satan Plots His Strategy to Coerce the Couple into Sin | *Trochaic Octameter* | 165
Satan's Soliloquy: Reveling in His Coming Duplicity | *Villanelle* | 167
Eve Insists that She Work Alone to be More Productive | *Iambic Hexameter* | 169
Satan Stalks Eve in the Garden | *Dactylic Nonameter* | 170
Satan Lures Eve to the Forbidden Tree | *Common Meter* | 173
Satan Speaks Seductively to Eve | *Iambic Pentameter* | 175
Eve Starts to Yield | *Anapestic Decameter* | 176
Eve Surrenders to Sin | *Anapestic Dimeter* | 177
Eve Tries to Seduce Adam | *Anapestic Decameter* | 178
Adam Begins to Give In | *Dizain* | 180
Adam and Eve Sin Together | *Iambic Pentameter* | 182
Adam and Eve Blame Each Other | *Trochaic Heptameter* | 184

10 | Adam and Eve Exhibit Shame. Sin and Death Come to Earth. God Allows Earth to Experience Disorder.

God the Father and Son Consider the Aftermath | *Shakespearean Sonnet* | 189
God the Son Confronts Adam and Eve | *Iambic Tetrameter* | 190
The Serpent's Punishment | *Huitain* | 194

Contents

Woman's Punishment | *Quintain* | 195
Man's Punishment | *Quintilla* | 196
The Loss of Innocence and Purity in Mankind | *Quintain* | 197
Satan Meets with Sin and Death and Returns to Hell | *Anapestic Hexameter* | 198
The Demons in Hell are Transformed into Snakes. | *Iambic Hexameter* | 199
God Reacts to the Presence of Sin and Death on Earth | *Iambic Dodecameter* | 203
Adam Grieves over the Thought of Eternal Pain | *Interlocking Rubaiyat* | 205
Eve Despairs | *Dactylic Octameter* | 207
Adam Resigns Himself to Punishment | *Iambic Pentameter* | 209

11 | The Angel Michael Prepares Adam and Eve for Mankind's Troubling Future

The Son of God Has Mercy on the Sinners | *Anapestic Pentameter* | 213
Song to Sinners Who've Rejected God | *Rondine* | 214
Michael is Sent to Banish Adam and Eve from Eden | *Trochaic Octameter* | 215
Adam and Eve Sense a Change in the Air | *Anapestic Hexameter* | 217
Michael Appears to Adam and Eve | *Iambic Tetrameter* | 218
Eve and Adam Lament the Loss of Paradise | *Iambic Pentameter* | 219
Michael Begins to Reveal the Future | *Iambic Hexameter* | 221
Adam is Shown a Vision of His Sons | *Anapestic Heptameter* | 222
Adam Views Future Decadence | *Iambic Hexameter* | 224
A Future Filled with War | *Curtal Sonnet* | 225
How Human Depravity will Lead to the Great Flood | *Common Meter* | 226
Before Noah | *Zejel* | 229
After the Flood | *Sonnet* | 230

Contents

12 | Michael Continues with Visions of the Future. Adam and Eve Accept Their Punishment and Look Forward to Salvation.

Adam Witnesses the Tower of Babel | *Chanso* | 235
Michael Tells How Faithful Men will Deliver the Sinners | *Iambic Pentameter* | 236
From Abraham to Moses | *Anapestic Octameter* | 237
Plagues on the Pharaoh's Land | *Interlocking Rubaiyat* | 238
Moses Leads the Believers to the Promised Land | *Anapestic Octameter* | 239
After Moses: Laws and Lawlessness | *Iambic Octameter* | 241
The Coming of the Messiah | *Ottava Rima* | 242
Michael Explains the Power of the Commandments | *Trochaic Hexameter* | 243
The Second Coming | *Sonnet* | 245
The Lord Has Risen, but He Remains in Spirit | *Iambic Pentameter* | 246
Adam and Eve Depart Paradise with Hope for the Future | *Iambic Hexameter* | 247

Introduction

Paradise Lost: A Poetic Journey relates the epic story of *Milton's Paradise Lost* as a narrative poem, with numerous variations in meter and rhyme and the utilization of various classical poetic forms. Although a poem, the text reads much like prose. The narrative itself is updated to comprehensible modern language while retaining the spirit and essential detail of Milton's work.

John Milton (1608–1674) wrote *Paradise Lost* in iambic pentameter. *Paradise Lost: A Poetic Journey* alternately employs iambic (∪ —), anapestic (∪ ∪ —), trochaic (— ∪), and dactylic (— ∪ ∪) meter (where — is accented, ∪ is unaccented). Sequences of feet within lines include tri-, tetra-, penta-, hexa-, and beyond. (Meter and feet for each passage are noted in the Table of Contents.) Numerous classical poetic forms are incorporated into the text. These include one or more of the following:

Introduction

Ballade (French)

Bref Double (French)

Chanso (French)

Chueh-Chu (Chinese)

Common Meter

Curtal Sonnet (English)

Cyhydedd Fer (Welsh)

Decima (Latin American)

Dizain (French)

Espinela (Spanish)

Haiku (Japanese)

Heroic Rispetto (Italian)

Heroic Stanza (English)

Huitain (French)

Interlocking Rubaiyat (Persian)

Kyrielle (French)

Nazm (Urdu/Arabic)

Nonet (Italian)

Octave

Ottava Rima (Italian)

Quatrain

Quintain

Quintilla (Spanish)

Rime Couee (French)

Rispetto (Italian)

Rondeau (French)

Rondine (French)

Sonnet, Petrarchan (Italian)

Sonnet, Shakespearean (English)

Spenserian Stanza (English)

Terza Rima (Italian)

Villanelle (French)

Zejel (Hispano-Muslim)

1

Satan and His Allies are Banished to Hell

AUTHOR'S PLEA

Of Man's first disobedience,
embracing the *Forbidden Tree*,
a taste of fruit was evidence
of sinful souls whose destiny
was loss of bliss in Paradise.
A Godly Presence will restore
the gift of Earth: He'll visit twice,
and rid the world forevermore
of those possessed by lust and greed
and arrogance. Oh Muses, guide
me now, with words of wisdom; lead
me not upon a path of pride
in prose and rhyme. Let Providence
be recognized, and let my voice
reveal the realms divine from whence
the heavens hear my soul rejoice.

ANGELS REBEL, AND ARE CAST INTO HELL

Let me start with the reason that profligate souls
were seduced and deceived, and coerced to rebel
against Nature, to blindly abandon their roles
as the Seraphim, straddling the edges of hell

with their features askew in a menacing pose.
'Twas the serpentlike Satan who caused all the pain.
He arose from the darkness below to impose
his command over Adam and Eve, and to reign

over all of their children. But cast into hell,
to the flames of a furnace, tempestuous fire,
he was vexed by the thought of the angels who dwell
in the splendor of Heaven. Consumed with desire

for revenge, he was desperate. Darkness prevailed
in his dungeon of souls—even towers of flame
burned as black as the night! All the sufferers wailed
as the titanlike Devil arose to exclaim:

"Oh Beelzebub, brazen as I, let us fight
to the end. Never bend to the heavenly foe.
We will gather our valorous partners, unite
in resistance, and rule over Earth from below."

1:45 Hurled headlong flaming from the ethereal sky

SATAN PLOTS REVENGE

Beelzebub and Satan fought
together once, and misery
in hell engendered sympathy
for common cause. So Satan, fraught
with anguish from the judgments wrought
by God, collected all his hate
and courage to coordinate
a plan of action for a course
of war to wage by guile or force,
to rip asunder Heaven's gate.

BEELZEBUB QUESTIONS SATAN

The fiend Beelzebub, grotesque in mien,
encloaked in shadows, spewed a bilious stream
of curses: "We've been conquered! How obscene
to plummet from the realm of those who deem

us undeserving! Yet perhaps the good
of Nature overwhelms us. . .have we failed
to show the netherworld's transcendence? Should
we face defeat?" "Our enemies are veiled

in sanctimony," Satan said. "Delight
in doing ill! It's better that we reign
in hell instead of serving heaven. Fight,
I say again, to overcome your pain!"

With that the Prince of Demons gathered in
his breath, expanding like Leviathan.

SATAN FREES HIMSELF

A burst of frantic speed
propelled the Demon now.
He snapped his captive chain

and turned away to lead
his partner with a vow
of vengeance, to obtain

the forces deviltry would need
to smite its foe. "We can't allow
the gods in heaven to remain

the Conquerors!" And Satan, freed
at last, could now envision how
to reacquire his rightful reign.

SATAN SEEKS HIS CAPTIVE ALLIES

"Infernal world! It mocks and tortures me!"
cried Satan as he flew through mournful gloom
in search of friends still stranded in the tomb
of fire. "They'll all revive, most certainly,"

Beelzebub assured him, "when they hear
your voice!" So Satan came to rally all
his slumbrous cohorts, issuing a call
to arms with wind and flame and shield and spear.

THE DEMON WARRIOR

And what a sight was Satan with a shield
as round and massive as the moon, a spear
like mast of mighty warring ship to wield
against his foe, to stoke his darkest fear.

1:221 Forthwith upright he rears from off the pool His mighty stature

THE DEVILS ARE RALLIED

On lakes of fire the Prince of Demons came to free
his allies. Glowing, ponderous, ethereal,
he rose above the rebels mired in misery
since falling from the heavens, with their spirits full

of indignation. "Rise with me, you potentates
and princes, once esteemed as mighty lords of man —
be not forever humbled in defeat! The Fates
proclaim your rightful place beside me!" They began

to stir at Satan's words. Appearing like a swarm
of locusts came the dreary shapes of Dignities
and darkened souls, exploding from the sea of fire

and gathering from slumber, each inhuman form
unfolding spear and wing and falling to his knees
before the Master, who was burning with desire.

1:331 They heard, and were abashed, and up they sprung

DEVIL LEADERS

Beelzebub and Satan stood
and watched as fallen angels rose
like locusts on the grassland. "Good
has turned to evil, and our blows

will rain on heaven's royalty,
the arrogant elite who claim
to benefit humanity!"
Behold the leaders who defame

the works of God, who come adorned
with pomp and gold and quests for fame,
who thrive amidst the spirits scorned.
The first in line: a fiend whose name

was Moloch, king and deity,
exhorting boys to sacrifice
themselves in war, to heed the plea
of hegemons, with paradise

the prize. And second, Bélial,
the politician, smooth, discreet,
his empty words and vitriol
disguising patterns of deceit.

And Mammon, third, a man of greed,
designing rules and strategies

to flaunt his deviltry, to bleed
the poor to treat his own disease.

MORE DEVIL REBELS

And others: Chemos, wanton orgies, rites
of lust and bacchanal; and Astoreth,
whose virgins came to whet the appetites
of sacred harlots; Thammuz, facing death
each year for lewdness; Dagon, of the sea,
half-man; and Isis and Osiris, cast
from brutish memory of beauty past
to monstrous shapes and roles of sorcery.

1:344 So numberless were those bad Angels seen Hovering on wing under the cope of Hell

DEVILS ROUSED AGAIN

The trumpets blared and voices filled the air
as devils swore allegiance to the King
of Evil. Facing them with tears and pride
and rage, revenge was foremost on his mind:

"Immortal spirits, powers matchless, dare
we fight the Host of Heaven, He who cast
us down? I say to you, He can't divide
His legions, keeping some of us confined

in searing pain! Despair of peace, it must
be war—but not with battle gear alone.
We'll work in close design, by fraud or guile,
to triumph by maneuvering behind

their backs!" And now the shouts and fiery glare
revealed a horde of demons unified.

Blake: Satan Arousing the Rebel Angels

PANDEMONIUM

In a corner of hell stood a flame-belching hill
that was rich with materials, iron and gold.
At the urging of Mammon, they started to drill
for the riches his devilish dreams had foretold.

So the army of devils ascended the mound
where they ravished the womb of their mother the Earth,
mining silver and gold with the fury and sound
of the Cyclops, amassing a treasure trove worth

all the riches of mortals. They started to build
a luxurious palace adorned with the gold
they disgorged from the earth, and resplendently filled
and bejeweled with silver—a thrill to behold

for the spirits in hell! There were openings wide
for the passage of titans, and lamps burning bright,
like a column of diamonds. The splendor inside
was the artwork of Vulcan (who prospered despite

his betrayal of Jove). It was given the name
Pandemonium: *all* of the demons arrived
for a council of war, with a plan to reclaim
what was rightfully theirs. And as Satan contrived

his maneuvers for war, all the demons were changed
from titanic to tiny, just wisps in the air,

so that thousands of spirits, enraged and deranged,
could prepare as a group for the savage affair.

1:757 Satan and his peers. Their summons called From every band and squarèd regiment By place or choice the worthiest

2

The Demons Plan a Strategy to
Gain Vengeance on God.
Satan Begins His Journey to Earth.

SATAN ADDRESSES HIS ARMY OF DEMONS

As all the demons waited, Satan, high
upon his regal throne, began to speak:
"Poor banished spirits, you can testify
to endless pain and anguish from these bleak

conditions. Don't give up. We must unite
to get revenge. But first we must agree
upon a strategy. An all-out fight?
You know my choice: deceit and treachery!"

MORE EXHORTATION

Continued Satan, "We're oppressed,
but we're prepared to stand and fight!
Our rightful home was dispossessed.
We face a long and bitter quest
to quench our vengeful appetite!"

2:1 HIGH on a throne of royal state

THE PRINCES OF WAR, POLITICS, AND GREED SPEAK

The bellicose and spiteful Moloch rose,
expressing fierce resentment at the God
who cast him down: "I vote for war! Impose
our will! Deception is a poor facade

for weakness! Why give God more time to reign?
And why beware His wrath? He'll never send
us to a place with more horrendous pain
than here! It's better that you pray to end

existence if you're destined to remain
in hell!" Then Bélial, of wicked tongue
and stealthy spirit, countered with disdain:
"We'll never get revenge. In hell, among

our kindred souls, we have a small degree
of refuge. War might take us back to fire
and chains and burning lakes, and misery
like never known before! Our fate is dire,

but fighting makes it worse, since Heaven's filled
with guards. Impregnable, I'd say. Surprise
attack? No way. And what if God just killed
us off and caused our absolute demise?

At least in hell we're free, and left alone!"
Then Mammon spoke: "And what if God relents,

what good is that? We'd decorate His throne
with flowers, serenade with instruments

and hymns? How wearisome! Forgetting God
for now, I'd say we can't forget the gold!
With all the wealth surrounding us, it's odd
to think of waging war, to be controlled

by vengeance. Take the riches from the ground
and build a city made of gold! We're free
in Hell, we're slaves in Heaven!" So profound
were Mammon's words that now the destiny

of deviltry seemed settled. But the stage
was set for Satan's second-in-command.
Beelzebub would speak, and now the age
of true perversion seemed to be at hand.

BEELZEBUB TALKS ABOUT THE DESTRUCTION OF MAN

A silence fell upon the massive crowd of banished souls
as brash and boisterous Beelzebub began to speak:
"The thought of war excites you, and the thought of peace consoles
your spirits. But we lost before, and now we're slaves, too weak

to challenge God. We're not ethereal and virtuous,
instead we're princes trapped in hell. It's not a safe retreat,
we're stuck in bondage. Choosing war or peace is perilous:
no terms of peace exist with God, with war He'll just repeat

His victory. Our leader has a good alternative.
The world of Man is God's creation, and his masterpiece.
But less defended by his angels. Human beings live
in peace without the influence of devils to release

their baser instincts. Take revenge on God by ravaging
his greatest work, by tempting men and luring them to hell,
and hurling all His darling sons to us, and savaging
the sacred genesis of Man. Along the way dispel

your fantasies of kingdoms built in vain. We have to bring
an end to God's creation, casting every man to hell!"
And all the demons stood and cheered his words. Yet everything
depended on a volunteer to risk his soul and dwell

amidst the Chaos just beyond the gates of Hell, to find
the hidden world of Man. But all the demons seemed afraid

to venture near the armaments of heaven. "I designed this plan," cried Satan. "As your leader, I will not be swayed!"

PREPARING FOR A FLIGHT THROUGH CHAOS

The dark and silent flight from hell
would teem with danger: realms of space
through which the banished demons fell.
A task for Satan to embrace.

Some other demons volunteered
while seeking praise or saving face.
But testing God was greatly feared —
a task for Satan to embrace.

THE DEMONS GATHER FOR SATAN'S DEPARTURE

With Satan's mission firmly planned
the demon trumpets blared to heights
unknown, as fiery dark delights
possessed the whole demonic band.

For shame that men don't understand
the common sense of compromise
and concord! Devils organize
as one, together celebrate,
while men are overcome by hate,
the glow of conquest in their eyes.

A VIEW OF CHAOS

So Chaos now awaited:
    dark and limitless, between the realms of Hell
and Heaven, Satan fated
    to traverse the void through which his angels fell.

Beyond the demon border
    loomed a wild abyss, a ghostly blackened mire,
a chasm of disorder,
    fashioned not of sea nor shore nor air nor fire.

THE STATE OF HELL DURING SATAN'S DEPARTURE

With Satan now preparing for a rendezvous
with Chaos and a bout of demon derring-do,
the other demons, feeling restless, tried their best
to occupy themselves with feats of strength to test
themselves for coming battles. Others dug for gold
upon a rocky precipice, and then cajoled
the demon harpists for a soothing melody
while warriors recalled their acts of bravery.
And others sat discussing Providence and fate,
their just rewards, their wishes to retaliate
against a wrongful God. The most adventurous
explored their dismal world, across the tortuous
embankments to the River of Forgetfulness,
and further on the River Acheron, of stress
and sorrow, and the River Styx, of deadly hate.
And then a continent of ice, a constant state
of storms and hail and swirling winds—a fierce extreme
from fire—where souls were frozen in an icy stream
and then returned to flames, and then again to ice,
and back and forth till madness settled like a vice
on dizzied minds. Medusa guarded river's edge
with harpy-footed Furies. On an icy ledge
were hordes of Gorgons, Hydras, and Chimæras dire,
amorphous sentinels between the ice and fire.

John Henry Fuseli, Satan and Death with Sin Intervening, c.1800

SATAN APPROACHES THE GATES AT THE EDGE OF HELL

The edge of hell was ringed with gates
of solid iron, brass, and rock.
And fire! For Satan, now, the Fates
decreed a spectacle of shock

and horror: first, a woman (head
to waist), her bottom half a snake;
ferocious barking hell-hounds spread
about; and worst of all, to make

a lesser demon shake in fear,
a hulking shadow threatening
to battle Satan. Drawing near,
the shadow felt the brawny wing

of Satan raised to join the fight.
"Explain your loathsome, bloated form,"
called Satan, "black as deepest night,
and fierce as Furies in a storm!

You're blocking me, I need to reach
the gate!" The bulging shape replied,
"Aha! The traitor's here to preach
to me, like all the souls who died

in his rebellion! I'm the king
down here, so go away or fight

me now!" He started widening
his bulk and scaling up his height.

2:648 Before the gates there sat On either side a formidable Shape

SATAN MEETS A WOMAN-SNAKE AND AN AMORPHOUS SHAPE

The 'Shape' and Satan, face to face,
refusing to surrender space,
like thunderclouds at sea,
were halted by the woman-snake:
"Don't fight your son, for heaven's sake!
I'll let you have the key!"

SATAN HAS ENCOUNTERED SIN AND DEATH

A startled Satan asked the woman-snake,
"My son? This hostile, formless, vulgar shape?"
She answered angrily, "It's no mistake —
you've overlooked the incest and the rape!

Before you plunged from heaven, I was born
to you, but over time you planted seed
within my womb, and I was *Sin*, the scorn
of all, our son was *Death*. The wicked deed

condemned us all to hell, where I became
the Keeper of the Gates. I soon conceived
this scowling creature, with the very same
result—he raped me, even as I grieved:

and I gave birth to mongrels, and the ache
within my womb became this horrid snake!"

Blake: Satan, Sin, and Death: Satan Comes to the Gates of Hell

SATAN IS RELEASED INTO THE ABYSS

Upon her story being told
    the Prince of Devils put aside his wrath and quickly offered Sin
    his calm assurance that his daring mission was to liberate
    the prisoners of Hell, to carry Sin and Death above the din
    of Chaos, Night, and Discord on a cloud of fire outside the gate.

Said Satan, "From this dismal house
    of pain, I'll bring the two of you and all the spirits damned to hell
    to find a place of ecstasy, where new-made creatures live in peace
    and breathe the buxom air and taste the sweetest fruits, where you'll excel
    at what you do, where opportunities for sin will never cease."

Upon the end of Satan's speech
    his daughter Sin rejoiced: "Almighty God has banished me to Hell,
    I owe him nothing! You're my father, you're my love, forevermore!"
    She opened up the gates, and Satan gazed upon a rowdy swell
    of stormy blackened turbulence, unfit for angels to explore.

For there beyond the edge of hell
    a great cacophony of stunning sounds and voices, all confused,
    assaulted him through darkness. Only ruddy flames beneath the gate
    were visible, and Satan, pondering the void, appeared bemused,
    but then he quickly spread his wings, determined not to hesitate.

Upon the treacherous abyss
> a great collision bonded Satan, Chaos, Rumor, Tumult, Chance, and all the dreaded forces of the netherworld. "I'm not a foe," cried Satan. "Help me find my way. I'm flying through this vast expanse
> in search of heaven's light, to help my kindred spirits far below!"

Upon his orderless domain
> an anxious Chaos said, "I saw your army fall to Hell. I know your motive. Earth is near, so go and spoil and poison and destroy it all on my behalf!" And Sin and Death contrived a bridge to go to Earth, and Satan traveled on, enraptured by perverted joy.

2:949 so eagerly the Fiend...With head, hands, wings, or feet, pursues his way, And swims, or sinks, or wades, or creeps, or flies.

3

As Heaven Watches,
Satan Sneaks into Paradise

PROLOGUE TO LIGHT: THE AUTHOR IMPLORES GOD FOR WISDOM

Oh everlasting Light of Heaven, deign
to lift these shrouded eyes above the blind
and grasping gloom of Chaos. Help me find
escape from endless night. I pray remain

the veil of dawning mist, the cooed refrain
of mourning doves, a fragrance to remind
the poet of the forest pine, aligned
with breath of dusk before a cleansing rain.

But grant these beggared eyes a guiding Light,
the vernal lea abloom, a summer's rose,
a lover's fleeting glance, her smile divine.

Enliven me, celestial flame, ignite
my spirit, linger till your spell bestows
the brilliance of your heavenly design.

Blake: Christ offers to Redeem Man

GOD THE FATHER AND SON FORETELL MAN'S REDEMPTION

As Satan made his way to Earth, the heavens glowed
with God Almighty and His Son examining
the start of Man, and all the pleasantries bestowed
on Eden's children. And the angels came to sing

the praises of creation. God saw all of hell,
and all the past and future. "Satan has a plan,"
He said, "he wants revenge. And just as angels fell
away from blissfulness eternal, so will Man

succumb to sinfulness. Why not, you ask, create
obedience in Man? Demand their loyalty?
Because allegiance must be proved! To demonstrate
a love of God is up to Man. And thus they're free

to choose. And only by their choice will I be pleased."
Ambrosial scents suffused the heavens as He spoke,
and now the Son of God arose, and angels seized
the moment to rejoice while rising to evoke

a blessing from the Father's Son. "My Father, grant
your mercy on the souls of men, and shower grace
on those who fall away. Let Satan not supplant
divine benevolence with actions that debase

humanity!" And God responded, "Men are weak.
They're free to choose, but if they sin they must repent.

They must depend on Me, they have to hear Me speak,
they have to heed the special messengers I've sent

to them. For those who disobey and never seek
My help, their souls and their posterity are meant
to die! Their future in the afterlife is bleak.
Salvation only comes to men if someone's sent

to die for them! But where in heaven can we find
such love? To die for Man, the greatest sacrifice!
To offer up his life, to risk his soul with blind
allegiance to the will of God!" "I'll pay that price

on your behalf!" the Son proclaimed. "Let Death decree
My end. Because of You I'll gain eternal life,
and I will rise again to share the majesty
of heaven. Father, help Me end the bitter strife

with Satan, Sin, and Death! For each I'll seal a grave!
And fallen souls can seek redemption through my death!"
A host of angels praised the Holy One who gave
so much to please his Father. Never had the breadth

of sacrifice exceeded this! And God replied
with pride: "My Son, the destiny of Man depends
on you. Through virgin birth shall you be sanctified
as holy in the eyes of Man. If Man commends

his life to you, redemption follows. You will die
a man, but you'll remain my son. On Judgment Day
you'll raise aloft the penitents to glorify
their God, while unrepentant souls are cast away!"

SONG OF JUDGMENT

On Judgment Day the souls will come
    from Heaven, Hell, and Earth.
They'll gather for a tribunal
    to probe and gauge the worth
of all the living and the dead,
    a day of joy or doom.
And Hell, her numbers full, shall sink
    beneath Satanic gloom,
forever shut. The World will burn,
    and from her ashes spring
a joyous Earth that thrives without
    the sceptre of a king.

THE ANGELS REJOICE

Angels were thrilled and consumed with delight,
    and their crowns, amply filled
      with embellishments
bright as the blossoms of morn and the gleam
    on the River of Bliss
      and the amaranth
stream, were presented to God with the sound
    of acclaim for the
      Infinite One. He
exuded a radiance blinding the eyes
    of the Seraphim, all
      of whom gathered to
rise before God and His Son as the harps
    on the azure were
      strummed by the Cherubim.

3:348 Heaven rung With jubilee, and loud Hosannas filled The eternal regions.

SATAN FLIES THROUGH CHAOS TOWARD THE EARTH

In Chaos, in the darkness, in the waste
and wild and frown of Night, the start of life
was yet to come, in boundless space displaced
from Heaven, empty yet of calm and strife.

On windy seas of darkness Satan stood
and watched in silence, till a light appeared.
He followed it to Earth, a place where good
and guiltless Godly people could be steered

to him through sins of vanity and greed.
The sinners, pilgrim to philosopher,
might feel their saintly garb had guaranteed
salvation. But their pride would just incur

their punishment as cowls and cassocks, beads,
indulgences and chants and other tools
of fraud were stripped away. Such pretense leads
to Limbo, to the Paradise of Fools.

JACOB'S LADDER

From dark of dawn another beam of light
distracted Satan: rows of gems and gold
adorned a stairway—such a stunning sight

was never seen, a secret to behold,
the ends of Jacob's Ladder, jeweled gate
between the Earth and Heaven that foretold

the greatest act of mercy: to await
the penitents who welcome Judgment Day
as God's reward. But Satan's endless hate

prevailed. Beyond the gated passageway
he sought the star that warmed the Earth, whose bright
and bold appearance cast the night away.

William Blake, Jacob's Dream, 1805

AN ANGEL APPEARS

A star, the sun, magnetic beam
that warms the Earth, a dazzling stone
philosophers can only dream
about, secretes elixirs grown

from wonder, painting colors rare
and brilliant. In the crystal air
appears an angel, luminous,
contemplative, mysterious.

SATAN DISGUISES HIMSELF AS A CHERUB

As Satan traveled on his way
    he watched the angel, golden halo, winged,
    and clothed in white.

The Demon planned a strategy:
    his wayward journey might be clarified
    by clever slight

of hand and change of mien
    to cherub-like appearance, flowing hair
    and coronet and bright

and colored plumes for wings,
    his stature proud and regal, silver wand
    in hand. To his delight

the angel—*Ur*-i-el,
    a heavenly protector, Satan knew —
    was spellbound by the sight

of such an apt disguise.
    Unknowingly the angel turned to ask
    the Demon how he might

assist, and Satan said,
    "I'm seeking God's creations—Earth and Man.
    Please guide me in my flight."

SATAN DECEIVES THE ANGEL

So spoke the false dissembler, unperceived his lies,
for neither Man nor Seraphim can recognize

deceit. So Uriel succumbed to trickery,
and he exclaimed to Satan, "Let the majesty

of God's creation be revealed to dutiful
believers like yourself! His works are beautiful,

divine, incomprehensible! For I was there
before the Earth was formed, when angels, unaware

of His intent to shape the earth and fire and air
and water, watched the light descend the golden stair

to reach the Earth, the seat of Man, one hemisphere
in daylight, one beneath the moon at night. And here

He'd nurture man and woman in a Paradise
from which their progeny would bloom!" "Your words entice

me," Satan slyly answered. "Kindly point the way!"
And Satan's crafty plan, to flatter and betray

the trusting angel, was successful. Hints of mirth
accompanied the Demon on his way to Earth.

3:739 toward the coast of Earth beneath, And then he flew down towards Earth Down from the ecliptic, sped with hoped success, Throws his steep flight in many an aerie wheel

4

Satan Draws Closer to God's Children in Eden

SATAN QUESTIONS HIMSELF

For man and woman, Satan's imminent
arrival meant disruption of their peace
in Paradise, for Satan would release
demonic waves of poisonous intent.

But now the scheming Devil had to pause:
How beautiful was Earth! How bright the sun
that warmed the garden's soil! "Great work was done
with*out* me!" Satan told himself. "The cause

of my expulsion was my reckless pride
and raw ambition! How can God forgive
a fallen angel when perversions fill

his soul?" No longer could the Demon hide
the truth, no longer could he hope to live
in Godly bliss. His plight was Heaven's will.

4:73 Me miserable! which way shall I fly Infinite wrauth and infinite despair?

SATAN'S SOLILOQUY: BEMOANING HIS PLIGHT

Inhabitants of Earth must realize
a secret foe is planning their demise.

That foe is me, to wreak on Man my wrath,
to bare my boiling breast, to terrorize

the innocents. But heed the blazing Sun,
whose golden presence blinds the countless eyes

of stars. How much I hate that flaming orb,
how cruelly it seems to emphasize

my fall, my fight against the matchless King.
But why? He seems a gracious God who tries

to serve His faithful. Yet the good in Him
has proven ill in me! I agonize

because of this! And jealous, greedy, vile
ambition seizes me and satisfies

my savage instincts! Better I was born
a lesser angel. . .yet my brethren rise

to greatness and remain unshaken in
their loyalty! Why me? What justifies

*such evil? Maybe I'll repent. But no,
my Punisher will surely recognize*

*hypocrisy! And then a lower hell
awaits me! Hope is gone—I think it's wise*

*to reign as king of wickedness and sin,
to stand against the Kingdom in the Skies!*

The passion in the demon—anger, ire,
despair—appeared by now to compromise

his visage. Uriel was watching, and
began to sense a devil in disguise.

SATAN IS OVERWHELMED BY EDEN'S BEAUTY

So Satan stood near Paradise
beside the lavish greenery
and pinkish blossoms, fruity spice
and balmy air, a potpourri

of pine and palm, a sylvan scene,
a rainbow in the sky, a sea
of grasses, pérfumed air, serene
and secretive, a pageantry

of palette, fragrance, hymn, and hue,
the Tree of Knowledge, Tree of Life,
and crystal rivers running through
the center. Eden, free of strife,

devoid of shame, eternal Spring,
the work of God. The Demon's pride
commanded him: he took to wing
to pass the gate and come inside.

The splendor was enhanced inside,
with fountains, orchards, valleys stained
in rosy shades and magnified
by earthy scents as daylight waned.

But now, with wicked irony,
the demon witnessed life and planned

for death: let all of Heaven see
the damage done by Satan's hand!

4:172 Now to the ascent of that steep savage hill Satan had journeyed on, pensive and slow

EVE AND ADAM IN THE GARDEN OF EDEN

In the Garden of Eden the couple were happy, content
and protected, unblushing and natural, stewards of land
and the keepers of beasts, as the nourishing nectars were sent
from the fruit-laden trees to their rose petal bed through the hand

of their Maker. Though naked in front of the Heavenly Host,
not the least bit of shame was within them. Their flaxen gold hair
fell in delicate billowing waves—like a veil shrouding most
of the woman. On soft downy grass in the fruit-scented air

they reclined, and they dined, while surrounded by beasts of the Earth,
gentle beasts, tame and grazing, avoiding the garden where seed
had been laid. After praying to God, in a moment of mirth
they descended a hillside to wade in a stream. And indeed

they were happy. As Eve held him close Adam leaned to her ear:
"Gentle Eve, He has blessed us. But what have we done to deserve
such a gift? All He asks in return is our unfailing fear
of the tree baring knowledge of goodness and evil. To serve

our Creator, abstain from its fruit!" With a smile she replied,
"At the edge of the garden I woke to the sound of a voice:
'Heed my words, woman fair: You shall bear many children, preside
as the Mother of All on this Earth. And by making this choice

you'll have life everafter!' I turned, you were there, and you cried
to me, 'Eve, you're a part of me, near to my heart, at my side,

second half of my soul!' We embraced, and my spirit complied with the wisdom of God: by His words we must always abide!"

4:248 A happy rural seat of various view

SATAN LAMENTS THE COUPLE'S GOOD FORTUNE

The Prince of Demons couldn't tolerate
the Godlike creatures in the blissful scene
in front of him. Determined to berate
and punish them, he placed himself between

the herds of animals, his new disguise
a hungry wolf amidst unwary prey.
The joys of Eden made him agonize
with thoughts of Hell: "This couple, every day

enjoying gifts and pleasantries denied
to me! To darkened depths of Hell I'm thrust!
Perhaps the Tree of Knowledge is my guide
to vengeance. Stir the happy couple's lust

for sinful pleasures! Let them satisfy
themselves. . .they'll eat forbidden fruit and die!"

Blake: Satan Watching the Endearments of Adam and Eve

ANGELS CONFER ABOUT SATAN'S DECEIT

At dusk the angel Gabriel
was guarding Eden's gate,
and Uriel, approaching him,
was eager to relate
his grave concerns about the scheme
that Satan had employed
to fool him. Gabriel replied,
"I fear we can't avoid
an interloper taking wing
to circumvent the gate.
But if indeed he made it in
he'll face a bitter fate!"

4:589 So promised he; and Uriel to his charge Returned

AN IDYLLIC EVENING FOR ADAM AND EVE

In pink and purple came the night.
The couple reveled at the sight
of stars in clouded majesty.
Their labors finished, they were free
to nestle with the evening dew
and fragrant soil and shadowed view
of twilight. On the balmy air
were sounds celestial, sounds to share
of whispers through the olive trees.
Above their bed a gentle breeze
aroused the jasmine, lilac, rose,
and laurel, aromatic flows
of godlike gifts from playful Pan,
his rustic charms bestowed on Man.
And hymns of tribute would prevail
in serenade of nightingale.

4:335 The savoury pulp they chew, and in the rind, Still as they thirsted, scoop the brimming stream

A NIGHT FOR EDEN'S LOVERS

The blush of moonlight smooths the leafy bed
of Eden's lovers, as the icy face
of milky skies indulges their embrace
with teasing winks of gentle winds ahead

of blissful slumber. Angels barely breathe
in fear of stirring orchid-scented air,
till palettes pink and snowy blue declare
the waking dawn, and sylvan sentries seethe

with piney sweetness as the lovers rise
to greet their Maker with contented hymns
of praise. Beneath the Tree of Life they hear
the breezes seem to whisper this reprise:
Your children shall be plentiful as limbs
abloom when spring's ambrosial fruits appear.

Blake: Adam and Eve Asleep

SATAN STALKS EVE, AND ARGUES WITH THE ANGEL GABRIEL

The angels hurried down to Paradise to find
the evil spirit who escaped from hell and sought
to sow the seed of sin upon a couple blind
to his ambitions. Never had the angels fought

a demon so intent on vengeance. As they searched
the garden, north to south, for signs of deviltry,
an evil presence soon appeared, with Satan perched
beside the sleeping form of Eve, deceptively

embodied as a toad, and whispering his vile
seductions in her ear. An angel thrust his spear
at Satan and demanded answers: "You defile
this holy bed—who *are* you?" Satan didn't fear

the challenge, saying: "Not to know me makes it clear
you're low among the ranks of angels." "Look at you,"
the angel countered, "cast from heaven, you appear
as foul as sin, your face deformed, a lucid view

of hell!" Said Satan, "Any slighted soul would try
to seek a better place!" Now Gabriel drew near
and said, "No matter where you are, you can't defy
the will of God!" But Satan cried, "You need to fear

my boundless might!" Said Gabriel, "You're all alone,
your army's gone!" Said Satan, "I'm a leader, known

as bold and faithful, fighting angels on my own!
Go back to Heaven, sing your hymns around His throne!"

His taunting motivated Gabriel's reply:
"You're faithful? But to whom? Your vile, rebellious crew?
The bleak Infernal Pit is where you've gone to die!
Don't try to spread your sin and all its residue

to stain the Earth!" Exploding back to monstrous size,
the demon turned a fiery red. "Go back to hell!"
cried Gabriel, "you'll never win!" And Satan's eyes
were gleaming and his ghastly form began to swell

with bile and venom. God would have to intervene!
He flashed the Scales of Libra in the sky, to weigh
their chances on the battlefield. The fiend had seen
enough—he shrunk to normal size and flew away.

4:798 these to the bower direct In search of whom they sought. Him there they found

4:1013 The Fiend looked up, and knew His mounted scale aloft: nor more; but fled Murmuring; and with him fled the shades of Night.

5

After Eve Suffers a Bad Dream, Raphael is Sent by God to Warn the Couple of Satan's Treachery, and to Explain the Downfall of Rebellious Angels

EVE HAS A TROUBLING DREAM

In Paradise the dawning sun appeared,
and Adam was awakened. Eve remained
asleep, and Adam, helplessly endeared
to her, beheld her beauty and refrained

from waking her. He lay, half-raised, to gaze
upon her flowing hair and glowing skin.
With voice like Zephyrus in whispered praise
of Flora, Adam sighed, "My love, begin

your day regaled by roses, citrus trees,
and balm and bees and blossoms, all to greet
your sun-kissed eyes." "Oh Adam, how you please
me," she enthused, "but still, I must entreat

you, what's the meaning of my frightful dream?
A voice aroused me on a moonlit night,
and guided me until beneath a gleam
of light the Tree of Knowledge came in sight.

And there an angel said, 'How beautiful
a tree, how sweet its fruit, but no one here
to taste it! No one seeks the bountiful
rewards of knowledge! Won't you volunteer

to be the one?' With that he plucked the fruit
and tasted it, while saying 'Fruit divine,

forbidden here, is only meant to suit
the gods! Fair maiden, Heaven shall be thine

with just a taste!' And surely I could smell
the sweet aroma, so I took a bite
and I was swept to heaven, in a spell
of ecstasy! But troubled and contrite

upon awakening!" "Oh Eve, my love,"
said Adam, "tricks of mind cause wicked dreams.
Reality derives from God above.
Fear not. . .a dream is never what it seems."

Continued Adam, "What your mind abhors
in dreams will never be reality!
So cheer yourself, we'll pray and do our chores."
And Eve could feel renewed serenity.

5:12 Leaning half raised, with looks of cordial love Hung over her enamoured

EVE AND ADAM WAKE UP TO THE GRANDEUR OF EDEN

Their day had just begun
beneath a warming sun.
So Eve and Adam prayed
to God, and then they paid
a visit to the Tree
of Life. His mystery
appeared in every gift
His works bestowed. "We lift
our hearts and souls to you,
Dear God! Our world is new,
and yet it's perfect! All
the angels bow and call
your name! The morning star,
the planets near and far,
the clouds, the storming seas,
the citrus-scented breeze,
the soil, the streams, the air
have voices that declare
your greatness! Hear us, Lord,
and graciously afford
your bounty! If the night
brings peril, let your light
surround us!" Feeling right
with God, they worked till night
among the fruited trees
and vines and shrubs to please
their Maker, and to deem
contemptible a dream.

GOD SENDS RAPHAEL TO EARTH TO WARN THE COUPLE

Up in heaven an angel was summoned by God:
  it was Ráphael, sociable spirit and servant supreme.

"Something's stirring on Earth," God acknowledged with
  solemn demeanor. "The tranquil conditions are not what they
  seem."

As the angel bowed down in a pose of attentiveness,
  God told a tale of the Demon contriving a plan:

"All the deadly deceptions of Satan will soon be revealed
  in the form of temptation on woman and man.

You must warn them!" (Although in His infinite wisdom
  He knew that their freedom to choose would ensure their
  demise.)

Then a thousand winged spirits assembled for Raphael's exit
  from heaven to journey to Earth to advise

the first children of God of the Devil's intended assault.
  As the angels encouraged him, Raphael stared

at the faraway garden created by God in the center
  of cedar-lined mountains and streams. He prepared

for the journey, his wings held aloft like the mythical Phoenix.
  Through vaporous spaces he flew with the speed

of an eagle till angels in Eden received him with fanfare,
   aware of his imminent God-given deed.

Blake: Satan Spying on Adam and Eve and Raphael's Descent into Paradise

5:309 Eastward among those trees what glorious Shape Comes this way moving

RAPHAEL DINES WITH ADAM AND EVE

When Raphael alighted near the tents
of angel sentries, waves of energy
suffused the lavish garden, with a sense
of wonder for a Godly mystery.

Delicious fruits and nectars, plants and grain,
awaited Raphael. The couple laid
a lavish banquet out to entertain
their honored guest. A humble accolade

arose from Adam: "Such a glorious
and brilliant presence! Welcome! I'm afraid
we aren't worthy of your generous
concern for us!" The angel said, "You've made

a splendid household! Now the fertile womb
of Eve will fill the world—more numerous
with sons and daughters than the summer bloom
in all of Eden!" Eve was bounteous

with food and drink, and strong fermented fruit,
and she was nude, but Paradise was pure
of spirit, free of lust, of good repute.
And Raphael was quick to reassure

the pair that earthly food is sustenance
for human bodies, but the vital key

for nourished souls derives from Providence through inner fortitude and piety.

Blake: Raphael Warns Adam and Eve

ADAM QUESTIONS RAPHAEL

The food and drink kept coming: bread and meat
and liquor. Adam, still uncertain, said
"You're eating food of man, our meat and bread.
But why?" Said Raphael, "The food you eat
aspires to spirit, nourishing your sense
of being—mind and body work as one.
Obey, and when your time on Earth is done
you'll understand your spirit's sustenance."

RAPHAEL ADVISES ADAM

"Obey?" asked Adam. "But we *must*!"
Said Raphael, "No, Man is free
to choose. If you were *forced* to be
obedient, could Heaven trust
your true intent and honesty?"

Angel Prayers (unknown author)

RAPHAEL BEGINS TO RECOUNT THE FALL OF THE ANGELS

"I'd like to know about the angels who
    rejected God and ended up in hell!"

At Adam's frank request the angel Raphael
    reluctantly agreed to tell

his story, though it pained him dearly.
    But he felt the two of them deserved to know.

"Amidst the Chaos in the heavens, all the angels
    came to join as one, aglow

with orbs of golden light, surrounding God
    beside His Son upon a flaming mount.

He spoke: 'Behold my only Son, declare him Lord,
    the true anointed one, the fount

of wisdom, knowledge, mercy!' Angels danced
    and celebrated, joined in harmony,

and dined on succulent repast, imbibed on
    fruity nectars, gold and burgundy,

till rosy dusk brought all but God to slumber.
    All the angels hailed the jamboree,

except for one, who sat in silence,
    watching, waiting, weighted down by jealousy."

SONNET TO THE ANGELS CELEBRATING THE SON OF GOD

As angels gathered in a starry sphere
above the sacred hill, the Father blessed
His Son. Omnipotence was manifest
to heaven's edge: a venerating cheer

resounded, spirits whirled like galaxies
colliding in a fevered clash of light,
magenta nectars seemed to reignite
forgotten passions of eternities

of steeled obeisance, and the gaudy gold
of grateful twilight twinged the pearly dew
beneath the tabernacles. Flowerettes
and aery pillows courted and cajoled
the choir of angels to the dreamlike view
of gifts a loving Patriarch begets.

RAPHAEL RECALLS THE DOWNFALL OF REBELLIOUS ANGELS

The angel known as Satan was
    indignant, envious
of God and Son, and pondering
    a means of devious
revenge. At midnight he aroused
    his horde of followers
(a third of Heaven's Seraphim)
    and offered overtures
of conquest and destruction through
    a devilish crusade.
Respected as a leader, he
    was able to persuade
his faithful confidants to heed
    his words, to recognize
his discontent. And God could see
    these enemies arise.
He told His Son, "They're challenging
    the Kingdom, seeking war
against our sacred realm." The Son
    responded, "I abhor
the demons! Such disloyalty,
    and evil, and deceit!
Our faithful followers will drive
    the devils to defeat!"

SATAN RALLIES HIS REBEL COHORTS

With an army of angel defectors,
    the Demon (named Satan, once Lucifer) came
to his throne at the top of a mountain
    and watched as the soldiers kept calling his name
and reflecting their swords like the
    stars in the night or the dewdrops at dawn. Then he spoke
to his minions: "His Son on the throne?
    Can't we fight for our freedom and cast off this yoke?
Would you rather give up and go down on
    your knees? You're a Native of Heaven, you're free!
They assume with their princedoms and
    titles that rulership comes with a simple decree!"
But an angel named Ábdiel quickly
    objected: "That's blasphemous, based on a lie!
You're despicable, Satan, imposing
    your will on your innocent friends to defy
your Creator! You're equal to Him?
    No, His laws make us whole! With His Son at His side
He's more glorious still! So
    recant all your angry and venomous words and abide
by His will!" Satan scoffed at these words,
    and aware of support from the rest of his friends
he replied in a fury: "Creator? Who's
    that? What's the role of this 'Son' who pretends
to be Lord of us all? I'm his equal,
    self-made! So return to your king and explain
where we stand!" And his friends all
    agreed, leaving Ábdiel standing alone with disdain
for the traitors. "I'll leave you alone,"
    he exclaimed, "but the angels of God will await
your attack on His Kingdom, and
    heavenly justice is sure to determine your fate!"

6

Raphael Continues His Story.
He Describes the War between
Angels and Demons.

ÁBDIEL RETURNS TO HEAVEN TO REPORT ON SATAN'S TREACHERY

Ábdiel traveled all night,
    reuniting with God near a
cave with the marvelous sight
    of the darkness succumbing to
fields of Empyreal Light,
    where a squadron of chariots,
weapons, and steeds—all the might
    of the army of Providence —
waited for orders to fight
    against Satan's conspirators.
Angels looked up in delight
    at the presence of Abdiel:
soon he appeared at the right
    hand of God on the mountaintop.

ANGELS AND DEVILS PREPARE FOR BATTLE

"You served me well," said God to Ábdiel.
"Against a host of rebels, armed to fight,
your actions are a testimonial
to loyalty and fearlessness, despite

the absence of supporters. Truly, now,
a show of force is imminent. The end
is near for Satan's army. I'll allow
no disobedience! I need to send

both Gabriel and Michael to the front
as leaders. Take a million saints and thrust
your swords through godless rebels. Take the brunt
of their attack with confidence, and trust

me, good will conquer evil!" Then a cloud
began to darken heaven. Demons breathed
heroic, streaming far and wide in proud
and mighty waves, until the landscape seethed

with spears and armor of the enemy,
the hordes of Satan marching wrathfully
across the plains. And Abdiel could see
the Prince of Demons moving rapidly

across the field, his chariot as bright
as sunlight, ornamented gaudily

with flaming Cherubim prepared to fight
or perish for their hellish Majesty.

Said Abdiel, "You shameless fool! How vain
you are to battle the Omnipotent!
A single blow from God will make it plain
to see your actions are improvident!"

6:188 This greeting on thy impious crest receive

SATAN AND ABDIEL ARGUE

"You're a showoff," said Satan, "just seeking reward.
I'll destroy you! I used to believe we were free
up in heaven, unfettered by shackle or sword.
But you *all* became lazy, and happy to be

common slaves under God!" "Here, I'll show you a slave,"
countered Ábdiel, pointing at Satan's array
of disgruntled defectors. "Each soldier a knave
and a coward, and destined to lie in decay

in the dungeons of hell!" Then he leveled a blow
against Satan! The demon recoiled, and a cry
of dismay filled the air as a violent show
of destruction ensued in the storm-darkened sky.

6:327 Then Satan first knew pain, And writhed him to and fro

THE BATTLE BEGINS WITH SATAN AND MICHAEL IN THE LEAD

The angel Michael blew his trumpet and the war
was on, with armor clashing, chariots of fire
and flaming darts, the deafening incessant roar
of militants entangled in a smoky pyre

of random slaughter. Satan turned his vengeful wrath
on Michael, who exclaimed, "You've authored villainy
and suffering, so turn around and tread the path
to hell, where you belong!" "Your claim is fantasy,"

retorted Satan. "Routing you will make us free!"
The rivals clashed. With swords and shields against the air
like gleaming suns, the two engaged to such degree
that others paused for several moments, unaware

of enemies around them. Michael swung his sword,
and Satan's saber split in half, and then his side
was cut; and gushing blood, and writhing, he deplored
his vanquished state but covered up his wounded pride.

AN ASIDE

*A reader's note: an angel can't be killed
except by failure of the spirit, sense,
and intellect. So Satan simply willed
himself to health with grit and confidence.*

THE DEMONS DEVELOP A NEW WEAPON

Satan saw the landscape strewn with
    broken chariots and arms, and
dying steeds. And very soon the
    Godly troops would take advantage
of the weakened rebels. Night brought
    cover. Satan reasoned, "Heaven's
army couldn't win the fight! We
    need more weapons, though. More deadly
weapons!" Clever planning led to
    this: "The metals underground can
make a cannonball! Embed it
    in a hollow log and light it
with a reed." The devils raved at
    Satan's ingenuity. (They
dully wondered if depraved and
    lethal armaments would plague the
future world of humans.) Work was
    started on the cannons: reeds were
taken from the earthy murk, and
    minerals from caves and caverns.

6:406 Now Night her course began

THE DEMONS DEPLOY A DEADLY CANNON

The morning brought a readiness
    to heaven's angels. Soon a cry
rang out: "To arms! The foe's at hand!"
    The demon army lurked nearby,

returning now to stand behind
    their leader, Satan. They arrived
with shrewdly feigned displays of peace,
    but strange machinery revived

distrust among the Godly host.
    Indeed, a triple mounted row
of hollowed logs was pointed at
    the heavens while the doomful glow

of burning reeds prepared to light
    the ends. A great explosive roar
disgorged a flaming fusillade
    of heavy metal balls that tore

apart the battleground and felled
    a thousand angels; many more
were stunned or panicked by this new
    and merciless device of war.

6:410 On the foughten field Michael and his Angels, prevalent Encamping, placed in guard their watches round

THE DEMON ARMY ANTICIPATES VICTORY

On the battlefield Satan and Bélial
   ridiculed heavenly angels
     with deviant glee:

"Did they welcome our gesture of peace?
   Are they down on their knees?
     Do they see what it's like to be free?"

So the demons were planning on victory,
   reveling, shouting, parading,
     and feeling immune

to a counterattack. But as Satan
   commended his soldiers
     it seems he was speaking too soon.

Blake: The Rout of the Rebel Angels

THE SON OF GOD JOINS THE FRAY

The angels up above were filled with rage.
Their love of God was driving them to fight
on His behalf. Returning to engage
the enemy, they used their newfound might

to turn a mountain upside down and hurl
it at the demons! Satan's army tried
to do the same, and heaven was awhirl
with flying mountains, only to subside

when God enjoined His Son, "Go forth and end
this war! Without your presence neither side
will yield. Let all the angels comprehend
your worthiness! Let all be satisfied

with my decision—you're the rightful heir
to heaven's throne! So take my chariot
and fly with flame and thunder through the air
to seize the soul of hell, to carry it

away to darkness!" "Father, how your praise
emboldens me! I'll take your sacred crown
and holy sceptre—armed with these I'll raise
a *hallelujah*, sending Satan down

where he belongs!" And saying this, the Son
of God acquired a chariot aglow

with gems and panoplies of color spun
from rainbows. Armed with golden quiver, bow,

and deadly waves of smoke and thund'rous flame,
with twenty-thousand chariots around
him, God the Son, determined to reclaim
the Kingdom, hurtled toward the battleground.

THE SON OF GOD SUBDUES THE ENEMY

When angels heard the Son approach
    they turned to celebrate
with raucous cheers, and Michael told
    his army to await

the coming show of strength. At once
    the mountains, flipped around
in heat of battle, flipped again,
    returning to the ground

from whence they came. A dark despair
    consumed the devil horde,
and wild with vengefulness they came
    with cannon, shield, and sword

to battle back. The Father's Son
    announced his strategy —
to fight alone! He showered flames
    upon the enemy,

a savage storm, torrential floods,
    the terror of a night
unleashed with fears unseen, until
    the devils reeled in flight,

retreating like a massive herd
    of dazed and frightened sheep.
But merciful this Son of God,
    allowing them to keep

their souls intact, provided that
    they cast themselves to hell.
For many days, as Chaos watched,
    the panicked demons fell

in clusters through the crystal walls
    of Heaven, opened wide
to manifest the wasteful Deep
    where wretched souls reside.

6:871 Nine days they fell; confounded Chaos roared

Gustave Doré, Illustration for Milton's 'Paradise Lost,' 1866

CELEBRATION OF A MERCIFUL TRIUMPH

The Son of God triumphantly
ascended to a jubilee
of angels thrilled to glorify
the One who battled to deny
the wicked lord of blasphemy.

Yet cruel is the irony
that Providential clemency
allows the fiend to yet defy
the Son of God.

The demon's endless jealousy
will celebrate iniquity
and cause corrupted souls to die.
The One we trust to sanctify
our souls and guide our destiny?
The Son of God!

7

The Story of Creation

THE AUTHOR'S PLEA

Urania, the Muse of stars and planets, guide
me now! Invoke your sister Wisdom for support
and lead me back to earth, for I'm unsatisfied
with only half my story told. You must escort
me to the earthly Garden—darkness plagues me here
in your domain. So please embrace me and inspire
me, let me speak of Raphael and Adam's fear
of falling prey to selfish moments of desire.

RAPHAEL ANSWERS QUESTIONS ABOUT GOD AND CREATION

As Eve and Adam stood expectantly
with Raphael, their young angelic guide
prepared to counsel them. Said Adam, "We
are privileged you're willing to confide
in us, to teach us, and we're gratified
by all you do!" The angel said, "It's meant
to be this way, so God is glorified."
The words of Raphael were heaven-sent.

"So tell us," Adam pleaded, "what decree
from heaven made the earth and sun abide
by such a perfect plan? What mystery
of God's creation offers spaces wide
as Eden, airy as a mountainside,
and fiery as the starry ornament
that warms the Earth? My soul is mystified!"
The words of Raphael were heaven-sent

and wise: "The heart of Man should simply be
beholden to its Maker, to reside
in peace in Paradise." "But what degree
of grand divinity has justified
this gift to us?" And Raphael replied,
"My voice is offered as a testament
to God, whose chosen words I now provide."
The words of Raphael were heaven-sent:

"The heart of Man will always be denied
His mysteries. You'll have to be content
to see His works, to which I've testified."
The words of Raphael were heaven-sent.

RAPHAEL CAUTIONS ADAM AND EVE ABOUT KNOWLEDGE

Before he started, Raphael advised
the two, "I'm hoping you will comprehend
my words, as God desires. But be apprised
that knowledge has its bounds—you can't depend
on me to be omniscient, like the King
of Heaven. Knowledge is a lot like food —
in moderation food is nourishing,
too much impairs your body and your mood."

THE ANGEL BEGINS TO EXPLAIN THE UNIVERSE

After Satan descended to Hell
    with his legions aflame at his side,
the omnipotent Father exalted
    His dutiful Son and decried
the rebellious impostors who turned
    on their God. Thus did Raphael start
to explain the creation of Earth
    and beginning of Man, to impart
sacred knowledge to Adam and Eve.
    With the wisdom of God to assure
all the heavenly angels that
    Satan's disruption could never endure,
lofty plans were presented: the Son
    to establish a presence divine
in the Chaos, and peopled by humans,
    His children, a powerful sign
of His sapience, justice, and love.
    And the cherubs and seraphs and wings
of the chariots gathered to herald
    the Son, and the cymbals and strings
filled the air as the brilliant gold gates
    opened up, and the splendor and bliss
of the Kingdom gave way to the Son
    in the dark and chaotic abyss.

GOD CREATES THE UNIVERSE, THEN ADDS THE EARTH

"Behold the great celestial bounds."
By this the Son of God proclaimed
the edges of the universe.
And now the Earth and Sun were named,

and Day and Night; and once again
the golden harps and hymning praised
the Father and the Son. The sky
was firmament, of azure, raised

above the stars. The Earth was formed
but lacking life. To satiate
the needs of Man, the mountains, seas,
and plains were formed; to cultivate

the start of Life the tender grass
was clad in shades of vernal green
and sweet perfumes. The clustered vine
became a flower-filled ravine,

and copious the fruits that filled
the stately trees. A subtle mist
refreshed the world that God prepared
for Man and Woman to exist.

GOD MAKES ADJUSTMENTS

A pause ensued as God perfected light
and dark, and near and far: through human sight
the stars seemed smaller, and the moon less bright.
Creation was the Lord's, and all was right.

Jan Brueghel, *The Temptation in the Garden of Eden*, c.1600

GOD CREATES THE FIRST ANIMALS

Next (Day 4) came fish and fowl,
    and fox and wolf with stirring
caterwaul of praise and howl
    of freedom. God encouraged
them: Be fruitful, multiply:
    From urchin to the whale
Leviathan, from nestling high
    upon its leafy sanctum
to the songbirds who regale
    the dawning light to spell the
whip-poor-will and nightingale;
    the stork, the lofty eagle,
and the silk of swan and boast
    of peacock. Then Day 6, with
fuss and flair, begot a most
    delightful flow of creatures:

Albrecht Dürer, Adam and Eve, 1504

MORE ANIMALS, INSECTS, AND FINALLY MAN AND WOMAN

The lion, sinewy
beneath its tawny mane.
Behemoths: elephant
and hippo. Fierce domain
of scaly crocodile
and serpents—sinuous,
seductive. Honeybees
and ants in arduous
endeavor. Insects: more
than droplets in the sea,
some winged, some earthen-hued,
and some a tapestry
of colors. Yet the end
of all this work remains
undone: creating Man
and Wife, as God ordains.

7:387 And God said, 'Let the waters generate Reptile with spawn abundant, living soul; And let Fowl fly above the earth

ALL HEAVEN CELEBRATES. RAPHAEL CONCLUDES HIS STORY

Six days done, and God returns to waves of exultation.
Heaven's Gates are opened to the coming celebration.
Angels fete their King with harps and trumpets, jubilation
fills celestial days and nights with news of God's Creation!

Seventh day, a day of rest, and string and pipe are blending
in a dedication to Creation, voices lending
comfort to the gathering and Heaven's light ascending
to the stars for life to come, with grace of God unending.

SONNET OF GLORY: MANKIND RECEIVES GIFTS AND GUIDANCE

The Father deigned to fashion Man as lord
of all the birds and beasts and land and sea.
"Be fruitful, multiply—a great reward
awaits: you'll live in bliss, your progeny
shall fill the earth. But never touch the Tree
of Good and Evil!" Harp and dulcimer
embraced the Son, angelic harmony
of voices raised in song, an overture
of praise for seven days that manifest
the might of God. For even if the ghost
of scheming demons threatens to divest
the Kingdom of its blest angelic host,
the force of Good will overcome the bane
of Satan. God and Son together reign!

Johann Wenzel Peter, Adam and Eve in the Garden of Eden, c.1800

8

Adam and Raphael Finish Their Conversation.
Adam Describes the Gifts from God:
Paradise and a Female Partner.

ADAM ASKS RAPHAEL ABOUT THE ROLE OF EARTH

The angel Raphael had talked to Adam while he slept.
Awakening, the man began to thank him. "I accept
your words, divine Historian! Your speech has quenched my thirst
for knowledge. Yet I beg your kind indulgence: I'm immersed
in doubt about this planet Earth. A spot, a bit, a grain
beneath the Firmament and all her numbered stars. Explain
why sedentary Earth remains the center of it all!"
Thought Eve: "Too deep, it's not for us to know." She felt the call
of conjugal caresses and digressions from her man,
instead of cryptic talk. She chose the place where life began,
amidst the fruits and flowers, leaving Adam all alone
with Raphael, who said, "The plans of God remain unknown
to all of us. The fabric of the Heavens makes no sense
to mortal man. It demonstrates the Lord's magnificence!
You need to know that great or bright implies not excellence —
the Earth, not Sun, may prove to be of greater consequence.
Although perhaps the sun is at the center, not the Earth!
I'm guessing life exists on other worlds, for what it's worth.
But ponder not the thoughts of matters hidden far above
the realm of Man. Take joy in God's extraordinary love!"
He cautioned Adam to be practical. "I'll let you speak,"
said Raphael, "but understand I came from regions bleak
and evil. God instructed me to watch the enemy
in hell—to view your start of life was never meant for me!"

RAPHAEL REFLECTS

"Satan and the rebel angels fell
from Heaven to the depths of hell.
Behind the gates were sounds of
rage, lament, and torture
and debauchery,
the destiny
that Satan
wished for
me!"

ADAM RECEIVES A DREAMLIKE MESSAGE FROM GOD

"I was sleeping," said Adam, "and suddenly found myself dazed
by a murmuring spring and a shadowy wood, and amazed
by the number of colorful birds, murmurations in song,
and they seemed to be telling me 'Join Us!' Before very long
I was standing and talking and naming the flowers and trees
that I saw for the very first time! I was stunned! By degrees
I fell victim to dizzying images, one of which came
like a dream as a bright apparition that called me by name
and invited me: 'Come to the Garden of Bliss—I'm your guide,
this is Paradise!' Flower-lined walkways appeared, and I tried
to make sense of it all. There were fruits ripe for plucking and sweet
troves of honey. And suddenly there on the pathway to greet
me a Presence Divine had me down on my knees: 'I entrust
all of this in your name, from the mist in the air to the dust
in the earth, every blossoming fruit, every bird, every beast.
You shall savor it all with a single demand: while you feast
on the bounty abstain from the tree that brings Knowledge of Good
and of Evil. My sole and most sacred commandment—it *should*
be obeyed above all. Don't betray me by touching its fruit!
If you do, then your pain will be endless, your pleas shall be mute.'"

ADAM SPEAKS TO GOD ABOUT HIS NEED FOR A PARTNER

A holy spirit dwelt within my mind.
Along the path were pairs of beasts and birds —
I seemed to know them all! A world designed
for pairs, except for me? I felt these words
departing me: "In cheerless solitude
I'm standing here. Can someone who's alone
enjoy his life?" The spirit sensed my mood:
"What calls thou solitude? For you've been shown
so many creatures, all at your command!"
"It's not the same, they're all inferior,"
I said, "you reign alone, I understand.
But you're Supreme of All, superior!
For you can make a creature talk to you,
and *that* a mortal man could never do!"

GOD COMPLIES, AND CREATES WOMAN

And God was pleased, for Adam used free will
to seek a change in purposes divine.
As Adam slept, the Father would fulfill
His promise of compassion with a sign

from heaven. With a rib from Adam's side
He fashioned Woman—lovely, amorous,
a perfect partner. Adam, mystified,
excited, fully healed, felt vigorous

with God's creation blushing at his side.
Amidst the birds, the scent of pine, and air
alive with newfound blessings, Adam tried
to understand the ways of Woman—fair

and wise, companion to the humblest beast,
her wings of passion yet to be released.

Blake: The Creation of Eve

RAPHAEL WARNS ADAM ABOUT LUSTFUL BEHAVIOR

The angel offered Adam sound advice:
"Let not the carnal pleasures occupy
your mind and body, clamping like a vice
upon your soul." "I want to glorify
the Lord," said Adam. "Fortunate am I
to have a mate! Her grace and decency
will guide my love, so I can justify
my fervent plea to God for company
and sensitivity for all eternity."

RAPHAEL'S PARTING THOUGHTS

Raphael declared
that pure and carnal pleasures
*can*not be compared.

Angels do embrace —
with spirits pure, without a
body to debase.

Raphael was done.
In Paradise, the test of
faith had just begun.

8:652 So parted they, the Angel up to Heaven From the thick shade, and Adam to his bower

9

Eve and Adam's Disobedience

THE AUTHOR'S LAMENT

This lyricist will speak no more
of holiness, of Angel Guest
with man on Earth. I now implore
the reader: hear my words, attest

to wickedness and tragedy!
Sad Task! More troubling than to choose
the anguish of the Odyssey.
For this I must invoke the Muse,

celestial guide and patroness,
to offer her astute advice
about my promise to address
the fall from grace in Paradise.

9:99 O Earth, how like to Heaven

SATAN PLOTS HIS STRATEGY TO COERCE THE COUPLE INTO SIN

Night enshrouded Paradise, and Satan, banned
    from lovely Eden,
floated through the darkness seven nights. He planned
    to find a means of
sneaking back. He studied every bird and beast
    whose body might be
entered. "Ah," he mused, "the wily snake, released
    within the garden
near the children of the Lord. With me inside!"
    He hesitated,
marveling at God's creations, horrified
    by thoughts of burning
for eternity instead of savoring
    the verdant splendor
here in Eden, center of the glistening
    expansive cosmic
wonders circling Earth. Said he, "How sweet the hill
    and valley, river,
grassy fields! Such torment all these gifts instill
    in me! Deprived of
this, my solace comes from making others feel
    my pain! I'll take their
mortal souls. Within the serpent I'll conceal
    a demon's cunning!"

9:74 In with the river sunk, and with it rose, Satan

SATAN'S SOLILOQUY: REVELING IN HIS COMING DUPLICITY

To me such glory shall accrue!
With just a moment's trickery
the bonds of Eden I'll undo.

With dark intent and furtive view
revenge will show my mastery...
to me such glory shall accrue!

With acts of vengeance to ensue
I'm certain of my destiny:
the bonds of Eden I'll undo.

A slinking snake I'll enter through,
and once we live in harmony
to me such glory shall accrue!

With serpent now I rendezvous.
When morning's light has come to be,
the bonds of Eden I'll undo.

And when I see the mortal two,
I'll have my opportunity:
to me such glory shall accrue,
the bonds of Eden I'll undo!

9:182 The Serpent. Him fast sleeping soon he found, In labyrinth of many a round self-rowled

EVE INSISTS THAT SHE WORK ALONE TO BE MORE PRODUCTIVE

At dawn's arrival, flowers breathed the humid air,
an earthen altar honored God, and now the pair
began a day of pleasant toil. "So much to do,"
said Eve, "let's separate for now, the vines for you,
the flower bed for me." "Oh, Eve," said Adam, "dear
to me beyond compare, of course we'll persevere
to do our work, but we'll continue to delight
in Eden's gifts. Before too long we may invite
our children to assist us! We can separate
for now, but doubt is troubling me, for all the hate
and treachery of Satan lurks nearby—I feel
we're better off together." Eve replied, "Reveal
the truth, you doubt my strength of will? I promise you,
I won't be fooled by Satan's wiles." "I know that's true,"
responded Adam, "but we're stronger side-by-side.
Temptation's better met together." Eve replied,
"But why go on in fear? Instead, if we resist
the devil's tricks, we'll please the Lord, and we'll exist
in peace." "It's not mistrust that drives my hesitance,"
said Adam. "Even though we have no tolerance
for Satan, his deceit can catch us unawares."
"I feel," said Eve, "that facing Satan *now* prepares
us for the future." Adam knew their love was based
on trust. Before they parted ways, the two embraced.

SATAN STALKS EVE IN THE GARDEN

Eve hurried off on the breeze like the flight
   of Athena, but girded with tools
     for the garden, not weaponry.
Noontime repast and repose would unite
   the two lovers, and Adam would toil
     while distracted with thoughts of her.
Pity poor Eve, so deceived by perverse
   and unhappy events yet to come,
     with the serpent awaiting her.
Satan was winding his way to traverse
   garden hedges to hover near Eve,
     unaware of her solitude.
Then she appeared with the fragrance of rose
   and carnation, surrounded by palettes
     of yellow and lavender,
sensual, delicate; Eve seemed to pose
   like a goddess, as pure as an angel,
     and Satan was mesmerized.
Eve was a beauty! The Demon was thrilled
   to the point of forgetting his guile
     and his hatred and vengefulness.
Spite would prevail, though, and Satan was filled
   with a sense of confusion. "My thoughts
     went astray," he rebuked himself.
"Hatred has brought me here. Not to enjoy,
   but instead to defile! Here's the woman
     I seek, and her husband is
nowhere in sight. I am here to destroy
   them!" Approaching with wings on the earth
     and with eyes glowing red as a

ruby and head lifted high from the ground,
    he resembled the sinuous Nile
    as he rustled the leaves in an
effort to gain her attention. The sound
    of the leaves made her jump, and she looked
    to the side, where the snake appeared.

9:434 Nearer he drew, and many a walk traversed Of stateliest covert, cedar, pine, or palm

SATAN LURES EVE TO THE FORBIDDEN TREE

As Eve looked on in wonderment,
    the snake began to speak.
"Fear not," he said, "and harbor no
    disdain." A strange mystique
possessed the beast, and now his words
    were steeped in flattery.
"How beautiful you seem to me,
    angelic, heavenly,
a goddess, made to be adored
    by all!" And Eve was swayed
by all of this, but wondered how
    a snake could masquerade
as human. "Tongue of man," she mused,
    "imbued in one denied
a voice?" "Resplendent Eve," he said,
    "I wasn't satisfied
with beastly life, just food and sex.
    I chanced upon a tree
abloom with ruddy golden fruit
    all tantalizingly
within my reach. So ripe and sweet,
    I quickly ate my fill."
The trusting woman pondered this.
    "Your words betray the thrill
of tasting special fruit. Where grows
    this tree? How far from here?"
"Beyond a row of myrtles, near
    a stream." He hid a sneer
while reveling at his success.
    Said Eve, "Just lead the way."
He slithered on ahead. The tree
    of Prohibition lay

amidst a grove of leafy trees,
    but Eve could recognize
the one forbidden tree, the one
    that promised her demise.

SATAN SPEAKS SEDUCTIVELY TO EVE

"I'm not to touch this tree, by God's command!"
exclaimed an agitated Eve. "But why?"
the tempter asked. "If all the air and land
belongs to you, no need to justify

your wish to sample Eden's finest fruit!"
"But God withheld from us a single tree,
and this is it. You surely can't refute
the word of God!" The tempter's strategy

was clear. Like orators in ancient Greece,
he spoke in passionate and lofty voice:
"Oh sacred Tree of Knowledge, grant her peace
of mind, and make her understand the choice

is hers, to taste your fruit, to learn of Good
and Evil!" Then he turned to Eve: "Who told
you not to eat this wondrous fruit? You *should!*
It gives you knowledge! Never be controlled

by jealous gods who secretly suppress
your will to learn! So hear me now and taste
this fruit, and find your husband and profess
your love of knowledge with the greatest haste!"

EVE STARTS TO YIELD

Eve was moved by the words of the serpent,
    and hunger was drawing her close to the
    fragrant aroma of fruit on the tree.
"You are virtuous, doubtless," said Eve to the tree.
    "Even beasts sing your praises, and God
    gave you knowledge, but yet His decree
    has forbidden our learning—in fact,
    we will die if we try! Are we being deceived?
    Has the serpent not tasted your fruit?
    He has learned, he is wise. And he's willing
    to share with a victim of ignorance.
    Knowledge is surely a worthy pursuit!"

EVE SURRENDERS TO SIN

With her doubts swept away
she impulsively lunged
at the tree, plucking fruit

and consuming it all.
And her spirit felt free,
her resolve absolute.

And the Earth felt the wound
of an innocence lost,
as the angels fell mute.

EVE TRIES TO SEDUCE ADAM

When the serpent saw Eve with the fruit in her mouth,
   he proceeded to slink to the thicket,
      suppressing a sinister grin.
With her fill of the fruit, Eve was heightened in mind,
   as with wine, and she called to the tree,
      "Tree of Knowledge, each day shall begin
with my visit to you, and perhaps it won't matter
   to God, who has so much to do!
      As for Adam, what path shall I take?
Whether living or dead, we're together as one.
   I will tell him, of course! What I did
      with the serpent was not a mistake!"
And with that she awaited her mate,
   who was weaving a garland from flowers
      to place in her hair. When she didn't return,
Adam looked for her, finding her under the tree
   with the fragrant and succulent fruits
      in her hands. "I was wracked with concern,"
he exclaimed, but she spoke right away:
   "There's no fear to be had from this tree.
      It can open our eyes with the knowledge we need
to be one with the angels. A serpent who tasted it
   lives with the wisdom we seek. I beseech you,
      our minds will be freed
from the shackles of ignorance! Join me, my love,
   and our joy will be equal!" With that
      Adam stood with a look on his face
like the moment that irreconcilable actions
   inhabit the mind, leaving endless
      emotions of dread and disgrace.

9:784 Back to the thicket slunk The guilty Serpent

ADAM BEGINS TO GIVE IN

"Oh fairest Eve, deflowered and defaced,
how blithely do you choose to violate
the word of God! But love is not erased
by rashness. Never shall I hesitate
to come when you're in peril. Let our fate
be shared! We trust in God—to let us die
would uncreate the works that glorify
His name." "Oh Adam, how could I attain
a better love than yours? You justify
my actions even when your doubts remain!"

Blake: The Temptation and Fall of Eve

ADAM AND EVE SIN TOGETHER

"Not death, but life, awaits us," Eve explained
to Adam. "Share with me a taste divine,
my love. Commit your spirit, unrestrained,
to pleasures offered by this fruit, a sign

of hopes and joys to fill our coming days."
She handed it to him. Uncertainty
possessed the man, but Eve's seductive ways
prevailed. He ate the fruit, and suddenly

the Earth was moved again, as if to weep
at sinful acts. The couple swam in mirth,
intoxicated, reveling in deep
desires, in waves of lust unknown on Earth

until this day. "Such rapture have you brought
to me," cried Adam. "Never have I known
such rare delight! Forbidden pleasures ought
to multiply! A burning urge has grown

within me!" Eve was equally aflame
with passion. Hand in hand they hurried to
a shady bank where hyacinth became
a fragrant bed for wanton lovers who

engaged with wild abandon till the shade
of dusk invited them to dewy sleep.

But ghastly dreams of grinning serpents made
the night a horror. Sun began to seep

through greenery at last, but all was dark
in opened eyes, and nakedness and shame
replaced a time of innocence. The stark
terrain was set for argument and blame.

ADAM AND EVE BLAME EACH OTHER

Just as Samson and Delilah woke bereft
    of virtue,
so the favored two in Paradise were left
    dishonored.
"Foolish Eve," lamented Adam, "tasting fruit
    for knowledge
never gained! And now we're standing destitute,
    forsaken!
How can I behold the face of God divine,
    or angels?
Let me hide instead—oh cover me, dear pine
    and cedar,
gird my loins, oh leafy fig, to hide my shame!"
    They suffered
anger, hate, mistrust, suspicion. Each would blame
    the other.
"Eve, you wandered off alone, and now, despoiled
    of honor,
all is lost!" Retorted Eve, "It's *you* who soiled
    our honor,
Adam! Why allow my parting if your fear
    of danger
so disturbed you? Did my safety not appear
    to matter?"
Adam countered angrily, "Ungrateful Eve,
    you know I'd
die for you! You're blaming me? I can't believe
    your sense of
right and wrong! I warned you, but your confidence
    and willful
manner overcame my fears. I had the sense
    that nothing

could dissuade you. Such a reckless woman! Stray from me to
prove a point?" And so they fought until the day was over.

9:1121 Nor only tears Rained at their eyes, but high winds worse within
Began to rise, high passions

10

Adam and Eve Exhibit Shame.
Sin and Death Come to Earth.
God Allows Earth to Experience Disorder.

GOD THE FATHER AND SON CONSIDER THE AFTERMATH

The heinous act in Paradise was known
to God, and Eden's angels came to plead
forgiveness, thinking Satan might have flown
above the gate unrecognized. "The deed

is done," their Father said. "The will of Man
foretold this travesty. But punishment
is coming. Man and Woman spoiled my plan
to grant eternal life. My instrument

of justice shall be sent to Earth—My Son."
The Son of God responded, "Punishment
and mercy both, and justice will be done.
As mortal Man's redeemer, I'll be sent

to Earth, not once but twice, to dedicate
my life, which chastened souls will celebrate!"

GOD THE SON CONFRONTS ADAM AND EVE

With angels at His side, the Son
descended through a dusky glow
to enter Eden, where the two
disloyal people hid below

a leafy tree. "Come forth," the Lord
commanded, and the two emerged,
despondent and discomfited,
their once ennobled spirits purged

of self-respect. "We're naked, so
we hid," said Adam. Feeling shame
was new to them. "But now I stand
before my Judge to take the blame

for tasting fruit forbidden by
our God. The woman here, divine
creation, justified our choice,
as if by heavenly design.

I followed her, I shouldn't have."
The Son of God at once replied,
"Was *she* your God? She came to you
for love. Instead you satisfied

your appetite for sinful acts.
And woman, what is *your* excuse?"

Said Eve, "The serpent tempted me,
and somehow managed to seduce

me!" Hearing this, the Son of God
decided on a punishment
for each of them. And this would be
His just and holy testament.

10:100 And from his presence hid themselves among The thickest trees, both man and wife

Blake: The Judgment of Adam and Eve: "So Judged He Man"

THE SERPENT'S PUNISHMENT

The scheming serpent shall be cursed
and scorned. Forevermore he'll be
perceived by mankind as the worst
of earthly beasts. Beneath this tree
he's doomed to grovel endlessly,
his belly twisting in the dirt,
reduced in name to villainy
and sin, and never to revert.

WOMAN'S PUNISHMENT

Let pain be multiplied
for women who conceive
a child. And let the pride
and brawn of men decide
what women can achieve.

MAN'S PUNISHMENT

Let man be forced to work outside
in thorns and thistles, drenched in sweat,
his hunger barely satisfied.
From dust he came, and when he's died,
a tomb of dust he shall beget.

THE LOSS OF INNOCENCE AND PURITY IN MANKIND

Before He left the Earth, the Son assured
the man and woman, shamed by nakedness,
that skins of beasts and leafy shields would gird
their breasts and loins. And having heard the word
of God, their world grew dark and spiritless.

SATAN MEETS WITH SIN AND DEATH AND RETURNS TO HELL

At the gateway to hell Sin and Death stood in wait
    for their master's return.
Pondered Sin: "We behold the abyss, doing nothing!
    My son, how I yearn
to empower our world by connecting with Earth
    where our leader prevails!"
With the stench of the sinners pervading the air,
    and the blustery gales
and the mountains of ice in the chasm before them
    obstructing their sight,
they arose with their tridents and chopped until
    masses of stone to the height
of a bridge overlapped the abyss and extended
    through Chaos to Earth.
Sin and Death went across, finding Satan
    in hiding, his visage and girth
well disguised out of fear for the fury of God.
    But emerging with joy
at the sight of the bridge, he embraced both his kin.
    "As we watched you destroy
the self-image of man," Sin proclaimed, "we exulted,
    and hell couldn't hold
us, we're free thanks to you! Though rejected from
    heaven, you'll soon be extolled
as the monarch of Earth!" "Fairest daughter and
    grandson," said Satan, "you've earned
my respect for your joining of Eden and Hell!
    When at last I've returned
to the darkness below, you will travel to Earth.
    Sin and Death shall hold sway
over Man!" And expecting a welcome in hell
    he was soon on his way.

THE DEMONS IN HELL ARE TRANSFORMED INTO SNAKES.

When Satan entered Pandemonium, disguised
at first, he blended in with demon militants.
But then in blinding regal luster he surprised
the demon horde. At once his noble countenance

excited them. He shouted, "This infernal pit
is not for us! Possess instead a wondrous place
called Paradise, created for the benefit
of Man, but opened up to Sin and Death! Embrace

my words: through trickery the work of God was spoiled.
It only took an apple! What's my punishment?
Not much—the serpent took the blame! All sleek and coiled,
prepared to strike the foot of Man, forever meant

to slither on its belly!" Satan stood before
the crowd, expecting cheers, but shockingly a hiss
was heard, a dismal universal metaphor
of snakish sounds robust with scornful emphasis;

and now his arms and legs entwined around his form,
and he was prone and slithering. He tried to speak,
but hissed instead. The demon horde began to swarm
in tangled heaps upon the ground. Amidst the freak

display was Satan, python-like, the largest snake;
he led them through the squirming din, where spear and shield

were uselessly discarded, and a mournful wake
of hissing carried them outside; and there a field

abloom with ripened fruit, like that of Paradise,
attracted all the snakes, who wriggled up the trees
and plucked the tasty fruit but paid a painful price
when soot and cinder filled their mouths. Their hapless pleas

for water turned to hisses, and again and yet
again the hellish crawling creatures underwent
a transformation: first a demon, then reset
to serpent, always sibilant with sad lament.

Coppo di Marcovaldo, Hell Mosaic, 13th century

10:521 Dreadful was the din Of hissing through the hall, thick-swarming now With complicated monsters, head and tail

GOD REACTS TO THE PRESENCE OF SIN AND DEATH ON EARTH

In Paradise the hellish pair of Sin and Death
   had just arrived, and stealthy Sin
     instructed Death:
"Destroy the fruits and flowers and the beasts,
   and then your last and sweetest prey
     is Man—you'll take his breath
away forever!" God was watching.
   "Dogs of hell!" He thundered. "Blame the
     foolishness of mortal Man,
whose free decisions caused the filthy hounds
   to find their way to Earth
     to devastate My sacred plan.
My Son, you'll conquer Sin and Death
   and hurl the demons back to hell!
     And hallowed Seraphim, you'll cause
the sun to alternate the seasons, hot to cold,
   and force the winds to roil the sea,
     and change the laws
of planetary motion. Endless spring
   with verdancy and floral bliss
     is lost to Man. His choice
to disobey has led to turmoil in the air,
   from icy polar winds
     to tropic heat. The voice
of Man will vanish in the maelstrom!"
   Sin and Death were waiting. They
     attacked the beasts, and then began
their villainous crusade to spread
   throughout the Earth to systematically
     infect the souls of Man.

10:610 This said, they both betook them several ways, Both to destroy

ADAM GRIEVES OVER THE THOUGHT OF ETERNAL PAIN

For Adam, troubled seas of passion tossed
and turned within his mind. "An awful cost
for sin," he told himself. "Is this the end
of happiness? Deservedly I've lost

my blessings. My descendants can't depend
on me, they'll suffer too. I can't pretend
to think it's fair—Oh Maker, you create
a man from dust, expecting him to spend

his days as one with You, to celebrate
Your glory! Didn't you anticipate
my fall? Why punish others? Take me right
away, return my bones to dust. My fate

is in Your hands. But though my soul's contrite
I still exist! Though flesh and soul unite
in sin, perhaps my soul will never die!
Oh Maker, take them both! I'm filled with fright

to contemplate instead that Death and I
are deemed eternal! Maker, please deny
this horrid thought. Oh, what abyss of fear
surrounds me?" Thus did Adam magnify

his pain, with dreadful gloom, cerebral drear,
continued suffering for those held dear,

damnation in the endless holocaust
of hell, and all his hope to disappear.

EVE DESPAIRS

Lonely, disconsolate, Eve cried for Adam,
   but soon he approached with disdain
     in his countenance.
"Out of my sight, evil serpent! Unhappiness
   started with you. It's insane,
     even sinister,
taking my rib and becoming a woman!"
   With tears in her eyes and her hair
     all disheveled, she
threw herself down at his feet and beseeched
   him, "Forsake me not, Adam, I care
     for you deeply! By
hurting you, losing you, how can I live?
   I have sinned against God, but my sin
     against *you* makes me
see that the blame is on me!" And
   with that she continued to weep, and chagrin
     filled the spirit of
Adam, who said to her gently: "Again
   you are overreacting. Let's rise
     up together and
share in the blame and the suffering."
   Eve said to Adam, "I feel you despise
     me for letting the
serpent seduce me. But vile as I am,
   I am begging forgiveness. I need
     you to trust me, to
love me again. If you like, we'll be
   childless, and abstinent, empty of seed
     in my womb. If you

like, we'll seek Death, ending torment
    and misery. Death be not found, we'll succeed
    with our own pairs of
hands!" On this desperate note she
    suspended her plaintive remarks, for the deed
    was unthinkable.

ADAM RESIGNS HIMSELF TO PUNISHMENT

As Adam contemplated Eve's lament,
he reassured her: "Yes, indeed we must
repent our sins, but no, I can't consent
to self-destruction! Surely we can trust

in God to punish such an act! Instead
attack the serpent—through his bold deceit
we've nearly lost our souls. To crush his head
is our revenge! To spare him we defeat

ourselves! We'll tolerate our punishment
from God: to bear a child you'll suffer pain;
to earn my bread I'll work the soil. He sent
us clothed to do His bidding. Let's refrain

from foolish thoughts. We'll seek a refuge where
we'll spend the night in prayer, on our knees
beseeching God to rid us of despair,
to listen to His children's humble pleas."

11

The Angel Michael Prepares Adam and
Eve for Mankind's Troubling Future

THE SON OF GOD HAS MERCY ON THE SINNERS

In repentance the children of Eden stood praying all day,
and the mercy of God took the pain from their hearts in a way
that reflected the power of prayer. Restored to the Throne
of His Father, the Son felt the couple had sought to atone
for the sin of defying their Maker when tasting the fruit
in the Garden. "Let Man stay alive! I am sure his pursuit
of a better existence will come when I offer my life
as Redeemer, delivering sinners from deadening strife."

SONG TO SINNERS WHO'VE REJECTED GOD

Their Paradise is Lost. They vilified
His name. They've lost their immortality.
Distempered and corrupt they came to be,
and now, because His mandate was defied
they suffer punishment—they can't reside
in fields of bliss. For all eternity,
their Paradise is Lost.

But God's undying mercy will provide
a second life for those who faithfully
embrace His Son. For those who foolishly
reject His coming, heaven is denied,
their Paradise is Lost.

MICHAEL IS SENT TO BANISH ADAM AND EVE FROM EDEN

Angels blew their trumpets as their Father spoke
    to them in solemn
voice, "The man and woman, My creation, woke
    this morning sharing
all the gifts of Paradise. But now the taste
    of evil fills their
souls. They've disobeyed My orders, they've debased
    themselves forever.
Paradise is Lost to them. I now command
    you, Michael: With the
help of swordsmen from the Cherubim, demand
    their exit from the
Garden! Watch for Satan, lest he interfere.
    Reveal to Adam
what will come in future days. Keep angels near
    to watch the Garden,
flaming swords to guard the Tree of Life!" Prepared
    for swift descent, the
angel Michael deigned to heed the word declared
    by God Almighty.

11:208 the Heavenly bands Down from a sky of jasper lighted now
In Paradise

ADAM AND EVE SENSE A CHANGE IN THE AIR

Although Adam and Eve were afraid,
    thanks to prayer their sense of despair
was relieved. "All that's good comes
    from heaven," said Adam, "but God is aware
of our pleas and our prayers.
    He promised to grant us revenge on our foe
with a foot on the serpent! We'll live,
    thanks to you, dearest Eve, we will grow
in the eyes of our Maker." But Eve
    felt unworthy. "I *don't* deserve praise.
It's a merciful God who has
    pardoned us. Look at the beautiful days
He has given us! Thanks to
    His mercy and love we're allowed to remain
in this glorious Garden!"
    But Nature showed signs in the darkened terrain
under blackening skies that
    a change was upon them. The comforting peace
of the Garden was shattered
    as ominous breezes began to release
beastly predators seeking
    their prey. Adam bellowed, "A message is sent
from above!" And they watched
    as a menacing thundercloud made its descent.

MICHAEL APPEARS TO ADAM AND EVE

Upon a hill in Paradise
an apparition came in sight:
a crowd of angels gathered round
the angel Michael. Now the light
returned to cloak the verdant hill
in blinding heavenly displays
of Seraphim. And Adam spoke
to Eve: "I see a cloud ablaze
with light atop a hill. It's like
a great angelic Potentate.
He's standing solemn and sublime,
in military garb, ornate
and opulent." Then Michael came
to Adam, holding sword and spear.
He said, "At heaven's high behest
I bring a message. Have no fear
of Death, repentance will redeem
you both. I bring a more precise
and poignant edict from above:
You can't remain in Paradise!"

EVE AND ADAM LAMENT THE LOSS OF PARADISE

The words *You can't remain in Paradise!*
unnerved the couple, shocked them to their knees.
In audible despair they faced the price
of disobedience. Cried Eve, "Oh please,

we need to stay! To leave is worse than death!
These sylvan paths and shadows, flowers, trees
adorned with golden fruit! My very breath
is carried off by all the pleasantries

of Paradise, the sweetest sights and smells!"
With pity Michael said, "You're not alone,
your husband will support you." "What compels
your judgment?" Adam asked, a pleading tone

revealing his dismay. "Your tidings mean
departure from our home. How desolate
the world beyond! But God could intervene
if we are trusting of His infinite

compassion! If His absolute decree
can *not* be changed, my uppermost regret
is ne'er to feel His presence in a tree,
a mountain, or a fountain. He'll forget

me like the dust from whence I came!" Replied
the angel, "God is everywhere, on land

and sea and sky. You weren't satisfied
with Paradise, so now you'll understand

the wrath of God, but even in the bleak
and broken soil you'll find Him, still divine
and loving and attentive. Hear me speak,
He's everywhere, that's part of His design!"

MICHAEL BEGINS TO REVEAL THE FUTURE

As Adam pondered Michael's words, the angel told
him, "I've been sent to show the days to come as well —
the sorrow, joy, and fear. Ascend this hill, behold
the future!" (Eve, exhausted from emotion, fell

asleep. She stayed behind.) "Of course I'll follow thee,
my trusted guide, however painful or sublime!"
So Adam followed, ill-prepared to oversee
his coming days. It seemed that all of space and time

was laid before him: all the kingdoms of the Earth
for years to come, from Persia to Peru, from Greece
to Rome to El Dorado, glorious in birth
and turned to rubble in the end; from blissful peace

to bloody war. The angel asked the Well of Life
to open Adam's eyes. The man became entranced
by all the wonders. "Adam, ecstasy and strife
you see before you," Michael noted as he glanced

at workers in a field. "It's time you see the truth
behind your crime. How those who never touched the tree,
or heard the serpent, suffer in their guiltless youth
because of you. You've changed your children's destiny."

ADAM IS SHOWN A VISION OF HIS SONS

As the angel looked on, Adam stared at
   a shepherd directing his flock. In a field
just beyond was a farmer with bundles
   of corn. In between the two men was revealed

an incongruous structure, an altar
   of stone. Adam watched as the shepherd approached
with a lamb in his arms, as a sacrifice.
   Just as he started, the farmer encroached

on the ritual, smiting the shepherd
   with blows to the head and extinguishing life
in the man. With a feeling of horror
   and shock Adam knelt on the mountaintop, rife

with emotion, and screaming at Michael,
   "Oh, how could this happen? A man's sacred rites
ending up in his murder!" Said Michael,
   "They're brothers. You're seeing how envy ignites

deadly passions. And these are your sons!"
   With this odious vision in front of his eyes
Adam cried out again, "This is
   terrible, hard to imagine, my offspring's demise!

Will we all die so horribly?" "*Some* will
   be stricken," said Michael, "by famine or flood,
but intemperance—sickness from eating
   and drinking—is deadlier, more than by blood."

And a vision again came to Adam:
    a leper house, crowded with fever, catarrh,
ghastly spasms, edema,
        convulsions, demonic possession, diseases bizarre

and destructive, a triumph for Death.
    As he wept Adam looked to the heavens: "Why live
on this Earth if so wretched
        is Death? Are creations of God so forsaken? Forgive

me my ignorance!" Michael replied, "They
    have damaged themselves, not their Maker. Their will
is their own. They pretend to be
        Godly, but sin against Nature, and seek to fulfill

their own needs." Adam asked, "Is there
    no other way to face Death, to be spared all the pain?"
"Yes, by temperance," Michael
        responded, "not gluttony. Care for your body, attain

an old age, and you'll wither away
    without pain. Let quiescence inhabit your mind
so the ending is welcome." "You make it
        sound easy," said Adam. "You can't be confined

by your love or your hatred for life,"
    said the angel. "Whatever your time on the Earth
you must live with respect for yourself
        and for others till Death has begun your rebirth."

ADAM VIEWS FUTURE DECADENCE

A second vision now appeared before their eyes:
a flatland filled with colored tents, and great displays
of minstrels, organs, harps, and reeds to tantalize
a pleasure-seeker. Oddly, standing near a blaze

of fire were metal workers forging instruments.
A restless group of men stood waiting as a crowd
of women, gaily costumed, exited the tents
and sang and danced until the area was loud

and lively, amorous. The courtesans made love
on silken beds of flower petals, symphonies
of sound and smells and colors. Adam stood above
and watched as Michael told him, "Let this not appease

you, these are tents of wickedness. Your offspring Cain,
the murderer, has fathered them. The women, sweet
as goddesses, are harlots, tarts—they can't maintain
a household. All are atheists, and incomplete

without each other." Adam said, "It seems the woes
of Man are due to Women." "How you fantasize,"
said Michael. "Man's adversities and woes arose
because a man is selfish, lustful, and unwise."

A FUTURE FILLED WITH WAR

Another vision now appeared: a town,
a city, and a castle's lofty gate,
and faces flushed with war, a guarantee
of pillage, slaughter, booty, tearing down
the bastions where the bloodied bodies wait
to die in vain, as others valiantly
defend their city, flinging fire and spear
through choking air. An aging magistrate
appeals for peace and justice, but his plea
expires in sighs as no one seems to hear.
Hear Me!

HOW HUMAN DEPRAVITY WILL LEAD TO THE GREAT FLOOD

As Adam stood in tears again
    he voiced a harsh lament:
"So vile this human tragedy,
    so many lifetimes spent

destroying others. So much worse
    than how it all began,
with Abel's murder!" Michael said,
    "Ambition in a man

or woman constantly obsessed
    with thoughts of gems and crowns
can lead to plunder, slaughter, and
    the ravaging of towns

and cities. Look below at men
    who started battles, swayed
by avarice. But when the plague
    of war began to fade,

debauchery and revelry
    resumed, adultery
and prostitution, drink and dance
    and feast, a blasphemy

against their Maker. Clergymen
    condemned the travesty
and preached repentance, all in vain.
    A man of decency

and justice started fashioning
    a vessel for the sea,
a massive ark, with victuals for
    a great variety

of beasts and birds and insects, all
    in pairs. And when the door
was closed, the heavens turned to black,
    and rain began to pour

as never seen before, until
    the Earth was lost to view.
The vessel tossed on mighty waves,
    their crests a foulish hue.

The revelers were gone, consumed
    by monsters of the sea.
Survivors counted Noah and
    his closest family."

Again a cloud of anguish loomed
    as Adam saw the end
of all his progeny. He cried,
    "These images portend

the wickedness and suffering
    of days that lie ahead.
It's better to be ignorant.
    Or never born. Or dead."

11:729 Began to build a Vessel of huge bulk

BEFORE NOAH

The angel had identified
how greed and lust and hate and pride
invited Satan's genocide.

The sinners lived in luxury
with airs of smug hostility
for others, each an enemy.
Their self-importance was their guide.

And even those who faced defeat
to hated conquerors would greet
the crafty devil and repeat
the sins of men they once decried.

A Godly man will celebrate
with *life* when waters inundate
the land and sinners meet their fate.
The future thus is prophesied.

AFTER THE FLOOD

So powerful the flood that Paradise
is washed away. The ark, in aimless drift
upon the waning sea, begins to lift
as mountains reappear. In silence, twice,

a dove departs the ark, returns at last
auspiciously, an olive branch in clear
display. So Noah and his kin appear
on solid ground. They celebrate, the past

forgotten, hands uplifted to the sky.
And there, above the dewy clouds, a bow
of color forms, a sign from God that no

barrage of water shall again deny
the living Earth to Man. For God to show
His love, a Covenant He shall bestow.

Ivan Aivazovsky, Descent of Noah from Ararat, 1889

12

Michael Continues with Visions of the Future.
Adam and Eve Accept Their Punishment
and Look Forward to Salvation.

ADAM WITNESSES THE TOWER OF BABEL

As Adam stood in silence, Michael turned to speak:
"A second world of men has now begun. They fear
the Deity, and work the soil for crops, and seek
enjoyment sharing bread and wine with those held dear.

A man shall rise with ill ambition, not content
with fair equality. He'll claim an undeserved
position over brethren, as a testament
to arrogance. And those who haven't rightly served

him will be hunted like the beasts! And anyone
resisting faces quick and torturous demise.
This demigod will have his manic bidding done
by multitudes of slaves. You'll see a tower rise

to heaven's edge. But God observes the foolishness,
and in derision fixes tongues in varied voice
and language, till the workers face the sudden stress
of gibberish on puzzled ears! *The Maker's choice*

of humor has the angels laughing! Thus the name
'Confusion' comes to be." Observing all the din,
a disconcerted Adam hurried to exclaim,
"Oh witless man, his ego is the vilest sin.

He thinks himself a god with great authority
when all his godly plans are flights of fantasy!"

MICHAEL TELLS HOW FAITHFUL MEN WILL DELIVER THE SINNERS

The tale of Babel stayed in Adam's mind:
"The wretched man would starve for food and air
above the clouds!" The angel said, "How blind
are men like this. But truthfully, compare

his sin to yours and other men with free
and reckless reason. God will recognize
that Man is subject to iniquity
and sinfulness. He'll turn His holy eyes

away while looking forward to a time
and place for one devoted man to lead
his nation. Noah worshipped with sublime
intent, but his descendants chose to heed

fictitious gods. So God chose Palestine
and Israel to start, and promised all
the fledgling nations future life, divine
assurance of deliverance, a call

to arms against the devil. Then the great
Deliverer will bruise the serpent's head,
and patriarchs will rise to consecrate
the nations, and the word of God will spread."

FROM ABRAHAM TO MOSES

Of the patriarchs promised by God,
    first was Abraham. Isaac, his son, begot Jacob, who came
with his sons—twelve in all—to the country
    of Egypt, from Canaan. The youngest son, Joseph his name,
found prestige in the realm of the Pharaoh.
    He died, and the Pharaoh demanded the 'guests' be enslaved,
and their infants—male newborns—be killed.
    God sent Moses and Aaron to rescue His people. They braved
the abuse of the tyrant to seek a return
    to the land they were promised. But Pharaoh denied
the existence of God. He prepared to
    withstand all the hardships unfaithfulness likely implied.

PLAGUES ON THE PHARAOH'S LAND

The signs were clear, the judgments dire,
with hail and thunder mixed with fire,
and ghostly whirlwinds in the skies,
the breath of Providential ire.

And plagues of frogs and lice and flies,
as swarming locusts terrorize
the countryside and devastate
the farms and groves in ill reprise

to Nature's former fruitful state.
And carcasses disintegrate
from rot as waves of gray malaise
afflict the populace: their fate

is furrowed in the filthy haze
that sets their eyes and lungs ablaze
with dark and devilish displays
that sweep away the coming days.

MOSES LEADS THE BELIEVERS TO THE PROMISED LAND

The most dreadful affliction? The loss of
    the newborn of Egypt. The Pharaoh at last will release
the descendants of Jacob. But changing his
    mind he pursues them. Assuming their journey will cease
at the edge of the sea, he is shocked when
    their leader, named Moses, divides the great sea into two,
and the people of Israel (Jacob) are
    able to walk right across! As they try to go through,
the whole army of Egypt is swallowed
    by waves when the opening closes. With Moses to lead
them the children of Israel follow
    an angel illumined by fire in the night. They proceed
to the wilderness, safe from attack, near the
    mountain of Sinai, 12 tribes, and their God-given guide
in the person of Moses, with laws—Ten
    Commandments—ordained for the children of God to abide
by His words, and presented by Moses
    in violent storms from the mountaintop. Soon to be told
is the news of a coming Messiah,
    the Lord. To prepare for the Savior a table of gold
will be built, as the Ark of the Covenant
    binding the people with God. Seven lamps and a fire
from the Heavens will light up the tablets that
    hold the Commandments, to rule and protect and inspire.

12:237 they beseech That Moses might report to them his will,
And terror cease

AFTER MOSES: LAWS AND LAWLESSNESS

"Such stirring words are sent from Heaven," Adam said, "of Abraham
and all his progeny. For I was sad about the man I am,
about humanity! But still I wonder, why so many laws?"
Said Michael, "Laws won't pardon sin, but certainly they give you pause
before offending God. Though Moses brought the laws, it's Joshua
(or Jesus to the Gentiles) who'll restore your lost Utopia,
your Paradise. A pair of kings shall come, first David; then his son
of wealth and wisdom, righteous Solomon: beneath the golden sun
he'll raise a temple for the Ark of God. But after him a line
of foul idolaters will blight the temple, mocking all divine
intent. For seven decades Babylon will hold the sinners till
released by God. But lawlessness won't end, for that is human will."

THE COMING OF THE MESSIAH

The Savior King is born beneath a star
unseen before in Heaven, there to guide
the eastern sages coming from afar
to place their incense, gold, and myrrh beside
His humble bed of straw. And angels are
aglow above the infant deified
as King, begotten by a virgin birth,
Messiah for the godless souls of Earth.

MICHAEL EXPLAINS THE POWER OF THE COMMANDMENTS

Adam, flushed with tears, exclaimed,
    "Oh, thank you, Prophet!
Virgin, hail! Your son is named
    Messiah. Soon the
serpent will be wracked with pain
    from mortal bruises!"
"No," said Michael, "please refrain
    from talk of mortal
wounds. For any victory
    against the devil,
thwart his opportunity
    to stain your spirit
by obeying God's commands,
    the Ten Commandments.
God's own Son will have His hands
    and feet attached by
soldiers to a wooden cross,
    and slain for bringing
life to Man. Oh, such a loss!
    But on the third of
mornings after being laid
    to rest, He'll rise and
leave His gravesite, ransom paid
    for Man's redemption.
Thus the death you should have died
    is nullified, with
Satan, Sin, and Death denied
    the chance to triumph."

Blake: Michael Foretells the Crucifixion

THE SECOND COMING

The Son of God has risen! He'll remain
on Earth to meet His followers, to guide
them in their sacred mission: to provide
the news of Resurrection and explain

the meaning of Salvation. We believe
in life eternal! We accept the rite
of cleansing in the stream to rid the blight
of sin from wayward souls. And we'll achieve

Redemption when the Son retakes His seat
at God's right hand with Satan and his horde
in chains. But soon, when Mankind falls, remiss
in duty to their Savior, they'll entreat
Him to return to Earth, and He'll reward
His faithful and receive them into bliss.

THE LORD HAS RISEN, BUT HE REMAINS IN SPIRIT

When Adam learned about the second chance
to come, he wondered whether to repent
at once or wait. "The future may enhance
my bliss! But, also, won't the Lord's ascent

abandon His disciples?" Michael said,
"His Spirit will remain to help them fight
assaults from Satan. First repent, then spread
the Word and baptize sinners and unite

the nations under God. But there will be
evangelists, false prophets, men who use
religious zeal to gain celebrity
and wealth and might. Impostors will abuse

the laws of God. But once again the Son
will come, ensuring Satan pays the price
for tainting Man. And when His work is done,
the Lord will build a second Paradise."

ADAM AND EVE DEPART PARADISE WITH HOPE FOR THE FUTURE

"I've learned the greatest lessons," Adam said. "Obey
and fear and trust in God, believe that faith will lead
to Heaven's gate." So Michael said, "Your words display
more wisdom than the secrets of the Deep. A deed

of charity will take you to a Paradise
far greater than the one you must depart. You see
the angels at the gate? They know you sacrifice
your comforts in the present for eternity

in Heaven. Go now, waken Eve. And bring her cheer
with news of her salvation through a virgin birth!"
So Adam did. His words were able to endear
the angel to them both, for he had come to Earth

to offer hope to sinners. Now in bright array,
the Cherubim descended through the evening mist
to serve as escorts to the gate. The passageway
was brightened by a flaming saber that dismissed

the angel Michael from his mission. As they stepped
ahead the couple felt the hand of Providence
supporting them. With tears of loss and joy they wept
while facing days to come with hope and confidence.

Blake: The Expulsion of Adam and Eve from the Garden of Eden

12:645 Some natural tears they dropped, but wiped them soon